Dance first. Think later. It's the natural order
–Samuel Beckett

Motherhood: all love begins and ends there.
–Robert Browning

*The central struggle of parenthood is to let our hopes
for our children outweigh our fears.*
–Ellen Goodman

TITLE: **Another 'Pointe' of View: The Life and Times of a Ballet Mom**

DreamCatcher Publishing acknowledges the support of the Province of New Brunswick.

ISBN: 978-0-9784179-8-7

HQ770.P37A3 2008   649'.155   C2008-905839-9
Printed and Bound in Canada
Typesetting: Michel Plourde
Cover Design: Patricia J Parsons
Cover Photo: Ian Parsons

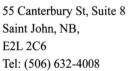

55 Canterbury St, Suite 8
Saint John, NB,
E2L 2C6
Tel: (506) 632-4008
Fax: (506) 632-4009
www.dreamcatcherpublishing.ca

Another 'Pointe' of View:

The Life and Times of a Ballet Mom

by
P J Parsons

DREAMCATCHER PUBLISHING
Saint John ● New Brunswick ● Canada

With Thanks...

This is my story. But there are so many I must thank for being part of it and for helping me get a story to readers who might find it entertaining or informative or inspirational or just plain something to think about.

First, there is my husband Art who played so many roles. He was not only a big part of the story but also an even bigger supporter of my taking the time to write this for you. Then, there are the many other wonderful people who were an integral part of the education of this ballet mom—many of whom you will read about. First, thanks to Barbara Dearborn, Mavis Staines, Carole Chadwick and Frank Augustyn. Thanks also to all the students in the 2007 graduating class of Canada's National Ballet School. I so enjoyed knowing all of you and I learned so much

Thanks also to Elizabeth Margaris for loving this story and taking it to the next step.

Finally, thanks to Ian, the dancer in my life. Being your Mom has been the most privileged experience of my life. This book is for you.

–PJP

Prologue

I've been waiting for the phone call for three days with an odd feeling of déjà vu. It's just like the old days, I think, when all this started. I always seemed to be waiting for a phone call. I thought we had come a long way. Maybe we haven't come as far as we thought we had. We used to be waiting for a school principal or an artistic director to call–or not call, since, depending on the circumstances, we might be hoping for one or the other. The control of my son's life and by extension our lives was in someone else's hands.

This time, of course, because of how far we actually have come, the call is from Ian himself. He is 18 years old now. The phone rings.

"Hi, Mom."

"How are you?" I ask cautiously.

"Pretty good," he says.

"Only 'pretty good'?"

Now I'm wondering if the much anticipated letter has not come yet, or perhaps it has but it doesn't say what we are led to believe it will say.

"Well," he continues, and I can almost see him looking around to see if anyone might be listening to him. "I'm actually very good."

I can feel his smile through the telephone across those hundreds of miles. I can't help myself; I'm smiling now, too.

"It came!" he says finally. "I'm going to be an apprentice in the company!" He's excited now. The "company" to which he refers is the National Ballet of Canada.

I'm bursting with happiness because my 18-year-old son has reached a mega-milestone on his way to achieving his ultimate dream. I'm proud because I'm his Mom. I'm giddy because I can now tell people what Ian will be doing when he graduates from the National Ballet School in June–because the inquiries are relentless.

"Could you tell Dad?" he says. "I've got to get to English class."

Tell him? I can hardly wait to tell him. I'll be on the phone in a nanosecond. We've all been through this together in a way, I think. But Ian has his story and I have mine. A parent's story is truly from another point of view.

Act I

*In which the ballet mom is conceived
and enters the world..*

ONE

Every Child is a Performer

A child sings before it speaks,
dances almost before it walks. Music is in our hearts
from the beginning.

–Pamela Brown

It is a world of beauty, refinement and grace where the women are ethereal wisps of energy, otherworldly in their movement, and the men are strong and sensuous. It is a world apart, something beyond mere mortals, and the only recourse for the rest of us is to look in on the magnificence like little outsiders with our noses pressed up against the glass.

At its highest pinnacle, it is also a world of struggle, pain that is both physical and emotional, a world of hard physical work and steely competitiveness unmatched in most other realms.

Neither picture is one where a mother places her child front and centre without some trepidation. Neither seems real; yet both exist side by side through that looking glass from where I sit. I know all this now. There was a time, however, when I most assuredly did not. I knew nothing about the ballet world.

From the very start parents think they know their children and have so many plans for them. Proud parents all over the world look at their little bundles of joy, and it strikes them sooner or later that *their* child is truly gifted. Many of those early gifts seem to be performance-oriented.

"You should hear him play that recorder!" says one mother. "You should hear her sing!" says a father. "You should see how she dances to every strain of music!" And so it goes.

Every child seems to perform at something. Given the opportunity to really pursue performance, there would likely be even more yet undiscovered gems than those who do make it into the real spotlight. But somewhere between that first sweet sway to the music on the radio and the corps de ballet of the National Ballet of Canada, the New York City Ballet or the Royal Ballet, something happens. That little something is life, as we know it: school, math classes, dating, practicality. Yes, every child is a performer and our Ian was no different.

But he wasn't a dancer–not by a long shot, or at least that's how we saw it.

We were typical Yuppie parents in a lot of ways in the late 1980's. A family physician and a university professor by trade, we married late. I was 33 and my wonderful husband, Art, was 44. We immediately bought a three-story stacked condo overlooking the harbour and one of the long suspension bridges spanning the narrows–not a place for children. We could even see those mythical red sails in the sunset from our third floor balcony. It was an idyllic first year of marriage.

Every Thursday after work we'd meet at the supermarket across the parking lot from Art's medical office building to do the grocery shopping together. On Friday evenings we always ate out. We were regulars at *Salty's*, a harbour front restaurant where we would sit in a booth by a floor-to-ceiling window and watch the ferry plying its way back and forth taking both commuters and tourists from one side to the other while we ate chef's salads and drank carafes of the house wine. We watched the changing of the seasons from that vantage point, and had serious conversations about books that we wanted to write together. We even managed to come up with what we thought were dynamite ideas for at least two of the books we eventually did write together. The twenty-something set may not have judged our life to be terribly exciting, but we were never bored. We loved what we did and how we did it. We could have been the poster children for the 1980's double-income-no-kids lifestyle and we loved it. Throughout it all, we considered the possibility of becoming parents and unalterably changing that life. At our ages, it would happen soon or not at all.

Eight months after the wedding, on a sunny Saturday in June, we attended a naming ceremony at one of the local synagogues. Our friends had adopted a tiny, blonde baby girl and we were honoured to be among the friends they chose to have with them on that morning. Brought up seriously Roman Catholic–and having spent my young adult life recovering from its aftermath–I had never even been inside a synagogue, never mind attend a Saturday morning service where babies were named. The large room was crowded and there was a great deal more noise than I had ever experienced in a Catholic church. Rather than all that silent praying and getting up and down from a kneeler that highlighted my memories of Sunday mass, there was more of a family feeling about it. If the kids got bored or agitated, there was no shushing: the parents simply took them for a walk. Everyone else chanting in Hebrew was either focused enough not to notice at all, or perhaps they didn't care. Either way, it seemed a refreshing–if a bit surprising–change.

I wasn't feeling my usual healthy self that day, though. The room was airless and crowded and the service was long and largely unintelligible to me. At least the seating was padded.

When we finally emerged into the fresh air we knew what we had to do. We got into Art's black Toyota Supra, a vestige of his long past mid-life crisis, and went directly to his office several blocks away. With few patients in the waiting room to see the doctor on call, it was easy for us to find an empty examining room with equipment for the test. When we looked at the result, we saw the blue line and stared, speechless for a moment, at the little piece of plastic that had just foretold a massive shift in our lives. Then we laughed. We were going to have a baby and we were delighted if a bit off balance.

Eight or so months later when Linda, my obstetrician, said triumphantly, "It's a boy baby!" we were 35 and 46 years old.

It was Ian and we fell in love with him at first sight. For Art it was his third time round; for me it was the first–and last.

Ian was a typically beautiful baby, frequently mistaken for a little girl with his mass of black hair and his big dark eyes. But it was his legs that gave us the most to smile about as he began to grow and develop into a terrific toddler rather than a terrible two-year-old. Never overweight, he was what one might politely call a pudgy baby with what we called his stovepipe legs. They were the legs of a linebacker if ever we had seen them! Not that we were particularly interested in his becoming a football player. As he grew his interests ran to heavy equipment and chasing a soccer ball.

But from early on, there was clearly something else in him. I was determined to know this child well and so was my dear husband. Like any late-blooming mother with only one chance to get it right, I embarked on a crash course on parenting, trying to educate myself as quickly and efficiently as possible. I read all the latest parenting books and vowed to give my son every opportunity to grow into a happy and healthy man. Art also had plans to get it right.

As a family doctor, after a quarter of a century of full-time five or more days a week and many nights and weekends spent delivering babies, Art had decided that the part he played in this child's life would be different. When his two older, now almost grown, children were very young, he had been very early in his career and had little time to devote to fatherhood.

True to his plan, when Ian was tiny Art began taking Thursdays off to be with his new son. After teaching a three-hour class at the university one Thursday I heard him calling to me as I came in through the laundry room from the garage.

"You have to see this video," he was saying excitedly as I dropped my briefcase on the floor in the family room.

"Okay," I said, bending down to kiss Ian who was sitting on the floor playing with a favourite bulldozer. He was about a year old. "What's it all about?" I saw the black cord snaking across the floor and it was clear Art already had the video camera hooked up to the television ready to show me something.

"I came into the room and he was watching the Youth Orchestra perform."

And there on Art's video was the evidence. Hands folded in his lap, Ian was sitting on the floor about four feet from the television screen absolutely rapt as the Nova Scotia Youth Orchestra performed a concert of classical music.

"How long did he sit there?" I said, surprised at the apparent attention span.

"Almost fifteen minutes!"

Although Ian had certainly been exposed to classical music, for I often played it in the car or as background music (Vivaldi was a favourite) when I worked at the computer, we had never considered early musical training. In fact, I had recently finished reading David Eldkind's book *The Hurried Child* so was concerned about the fine line between pushing little ones too early and not starting early enough. But even Plato is said to have mused that music is a more potent instrument than any other for education. Who was I to argue with Plato?

Did this child have a musical gift? Like some parents confronting a newly discovered musical interest in their child, we wondered about a little Mozart. But we truly believed that he would probably grow up to do things not unlike those that we did. A science degree or two, maybe grad school, maybe medical school–even law school would be appropriate.

But surely he could be permitted to be a bit of a Renaissance man along the way. A musical education would be a good accompaniment, we thought. After all, I had read the studies supporting a musical education as a firm foundation to understanding math and science. Oh how misguided we can be as parents! I suppose parents who themselves are artists must find it just as peculiar when one of their children shows an early aptitude for numbers and accounting.

But he was so young. Taking the middle way through the dilemma of how to best provide a young child with the ideal education, I enrolled him in Suzuki violin classes at the age of three-and-a-half.

I was told that this was the best age to begin. As the product of years of piano lessons myself–begun at age nine, carrying on for five or six excruciating years; never uncovering even a shred of talent–I was open-minded to doing it differently with my own child. After all, I knew at that point in my life that I'd never go this way again. So we went to the local Suzuki school and enrolled.

I had to do some research on this Suzuki approach to teaching music to such young children. I had a healthy scepticism about such early lessons, but I learned a lot by reading about it. I learned a great deal more through the ensuing experience. After observing how easily young children learn their native languages, Japanese music educator Dr Shinichi Suzuki developed a method of teaching young children using the skills of language acquisition–listening, imitation and repetition. Since the 1940s the method had yielded wonderful results according to the material I found at the time. However, I was unprepared for the reality of this listening, imitation and (God help all parents!) all that repetition. So despite certain misgivings about such an early start, we signed up-and I truly mean "we" signed up. Parents, I soon learned, must take part!

By the end of the first couple of months of lessons I began to think that if ever I heard 'Twinkle, Twinkle Little Star' again, I would run screaming from the room. Indeed, although I hold the belief that you can learn just about anything short of brain surgery from a good book, you can read about something until you're blue in the face but cannot avoid rolling up your sleeves and jumping right in. When it comes to this school of music, the parent has to get in there just as much as the bewildered child.

Every once in a while I'd think back to my experience with learning music. At the age of nine I had been sent to piano lessons. (My mother was of the opinion that to start any earlier was ludicrous. Since I had shown not a modicum of talent, that point was moot.) I have a vivid memory of my final encounter with piano lessons and all that they entailed.

By the time I was fourteen, I had been taking lessons for five years. Since my father was in the army we had moved several times, but it was my final teacher who made the most indelible impression; one that has never left me. The teacher seemed absolutely ancient to me, this view magnified by her eccentric old house on a tree-lined street.

To get to the front door, you walked up concrete steps under the deep shadow of heavily leaved trees. In winter, with the bare branches against the slate grey sky, you thought you were being pursued by so many witches' fingers. At least that was how it looked to the mind's eye of a pubescent girl who would rather have been designing and sewing dresses than going to a piano lesson. Then you had to ring an old doorbell and step inside to be swallowed up by a dark interior.

There was a grand piano in the window of the front room. The top was always closed and it groaned under the weight of piles and piles of music books, many mouldy with age. The room was dishevelled, smelled slightly musty on most occasions and seemed to reflect a lot of the personality of the main occupant. Miss Daley was memorable to me not for the music, though, but for three things.

First, she was dedicated to a germ-free piano and her wiping the keys with Listerine between students gave the room a kind of hospital-like scent that mingled with the staleness. My nostrils still flare at the olfactory memory.

The second idiosyncrasy of my memorable piano teacher was even creepier to me. She had a glass eye. Normally, even as a teenager, I would not have noticed a glass eye; my aunt also had one, although it was not apparent when you looked at her. My piano teacher's eye, however, didn't seem to fit correctly and bulged in a most menacing fashion, always staring at you as she sat on her low stool beside the piano bench. Several times she had placed a piece of transparent tape across it from forehead to cheek, giving the impression that if the tape were removed it might fall out. I tried not to look, but just as at the scene of a gruesome car accident, it was hard to look away. Years later I still had visions of that eye and how creepy the whole experience seemed. Every year at Halloween I'm reminded of that eye.

My third vivid memory was the one that resurfaced so clearly as I considered music education for a very young child. It was of the violin student she taught immediately before my weekly lesson. As I stood in the small dark foyer, I could hear the squeaking of the violin being played by someone who clearly had no more talent at that instrument than I had with the piano. I would often cover my ears to keep out the particularly nasty creaks. There and then I vowed I'd never give a child violin lessons. It was just too painful. Funny how things change.

Here I was, all those years later, renting a violin so tiny it was just right for pudgy little fingers, hands and arms. Once a week Ian and I took a private class. Indeed, both of us were required to be there. This seemed quite reasonable, although I soon began to realize that Ian would be spending the entire first year learning 'Twinkle, Twinkle Little Star' in various rhythms. He would stand there holding his little violin under his chin, looking so cute. Then the scratching would start. First he would scratch his chin, then his head, bow swinging about perilously. He liked taking the classes, or so he said, but there was something missing. There was no focus. However, the teacher said not to expect that. I suppose she was right, but the constant repetition of the same melody seemed to tax even Ian's three-year-old patience.

We had our classes on Wednesday afternoons at three. Each week as we went into the small studio, the previous students, a mother and her two daughters, were just finishing. One of these little girls, who was just about Ian's age but much tinier, would tune her violin before she laid it lovingly back into its case with the words 'fiddle case' emblazoned on the outside. It was one of those cute pictures that adults seem to find amusing; whenever a child who seems much too young to know what she's doing and just carries on as if it is what everyone's doing. Her mother smiled benignly at me, nodding knowingly. Damn, I thought, now that kid's really talented. It was only much later that I found out that the mother was a violinist with the local symphony orchestra and her husband was a cellist. Years later, when Ian was about twelve and the young lady in question thirteen, I discovered that little Celeste was something of a child prodigy on the violin. As soon as she finished high school, she left for Europe to study at the Mozarteum Academy in Salzburg.

If I thought Celeste and her mom were typical of the children taking these lessons and Ian and I an aberration, I was soundly disabused of this notion while attending weekly group classes, a required part of the program. It was part of the Suzuki method. It was these group classes on Sunday afternoons that finally got the best of me.

There we were, packed into a room three sizes too small for the group of parents and children. Some of the littlest ones lolled on the floor and chewed on their bows or their violins while others - the precocious little show-offs - stood proudly in the mandated circle and played. Ian was interested in the music, but wanted to do it his way. He most assuredly was not permitted to do it his way. The Suzuki School had its way and would make it Ian's way as long as he was a student there. I can't remember if I felt a sense of foreboding or not, but I certainly should have. It was to be a recurrent chorus in the song of Ian's performing arts life: *his* way versus *their* way with Mom and Dad caught in the middle.

It's early in life, I thought. There would be lots of time to pursue activities. I took the path of least resistance in this instance and took him out of classes at Christmas, claiming that he was not ready. Truth be told, Mom was not ready. We did take him back the next year and he even performed at the recital, his serious little face locked in a concerned frown as he clearly believed that the accompanist was playing the piece incorrectly. True to form, he scratched his head, bow flailing even in performance. We were proud of even that.

It seemed clear to me that the violin wasn't Ian's instrument. However, on the day I told his teacher he wasn't going to continue the next year she said she felt that he was gifted musically and that we should promise to bring him back to the violin when he was older. I told her I'd see what happened, still not convinced that the violin was his instrument.

So, as involved parents, we looked around for an alternative. All children should take piano lessons, shouldn't they? That's what my mother taught me. But before I even had a chance to find a teacher, an intervention came from an unlikely source.

During summer session that year at the university where I taught, my students planned a barbecue at the seaside summer home of one of the more well-heeled ones. They invited faculty members and asked us to bring along our families, so I took Art (who happened to be an old friend of the hostess's parents) and Ian. At 3-and-a-half years old he was the hit of the party. Few of the university-aged girls could resist our loquacious, happy and active little boy who spent most of the party chasing tiny battery-controlled sailboats as they motored around the periphery of the swimming pool. It was a gorgeous day.

Two weeks after the party the telephone rang at home. It was one of my students who had met Ian at the party. It just so happened that Gillian was working to make extra money for school by modeling and doing commercial acting.

"Professor Parsons," she began. "This has nothing to do with school. Would you be interested in taking Ian to see my agent? I told her about him and she wants to meet him."

It was a life-lesson moment. When an unexpected and unsought-after door opens to you, do you walk through it? Perhaps more to the point: Do you dare to take your child through it? Was this to be a key? There was only one way to find out.

TWO

A Look Inside My Heart

Your vision will become clear only when you can look into your own heart. Who looks outside, dreams; who looks inside, awakes.

–Carl Jung

When I was thirteen, I had one secret desire: I wanted desperately to be an actress. I fantasized about being in plays and taking on characters very different from the one I inhabited day after day. I auditioned for many school plays and was often cast in the lead roles in the early years. One of my favourite roles was of a character named Gloria Glamont who flounced about in high heels with her head held high and a sense of her own worthiness. I think she even walked around gesturing with one of those long, slender cigarette holders. She was glamorous and so far from my own life as a slightly geeky, straight-A student who carried what the other kids referred to as a 'brain bag' to school. It was a large leather briefcase, very practical to my mind, and very un-Gloria-like. Forever after that my father would refer to me as Gloria whenever he thought I might be putting on airs.

I wrote of my desperate fantasy in a little red diary I kept. It was one of those tiny hardbound books secured shut by a flap of faux leather that locked with a miniature key. Every thirteen-year-old girl had one at that time. Years later when I came upon it, but with the key nowhere in sight, I found myself taking scissors to the little flap so that I could rediscover the secret life of a nerdy thirteen-year-old girl. Even taking scissors to open a locked diary that I myself had written seemed a bit taboo. It was like I was invading the privacy of my younger self.

19

So I read the often desperate, angst-ridden words. I was surprised at the extent of my desire to pursue a dream of being an actress; I hadn't remembered its being so strong. My parents had supported my interest as good parents do, attending every play I was in, but it never once occurred to them that I would do less, or more, than go to university to study nursing, the subject of my grade four public speaking contest speech. I won the competition, too. Then I won it again the next year. Speaking in public and acting: they did not seem to be too far apart in my mind. Perhaps I did have some talent. But there's a significant difference I've come to find between an interest in something and a passion for it. I wasn't prepared to face the hurdles on the way to that acting career. I wasn't sure what that kind of passion looked like; I only know that when I took a close look inside my heart, it wasn't living there.

Then I evolved, as we tend to. First I wanted to design clothes. I was something of an early sewing wizard and I loved it. By the time I was sixteen, I had won several contests for outfits I had created. Later in my university days I would make ball gowns and wedding dresses, but talent wasn't enough. The passion that had seemed so strong seemed to burn down like a candle that has come to the end of its wick.

By the time I was halfway through high school I wanted to be a novelist and, although I hated my high school English classes and excelled in math and science, I did my special grade 11 distinction project in English where I was allowed to write short stories. I never really told anyone of my secret desire to write books, I just kept writing. So, all my life my parents supported the practical path, as it reflected their own choices in life; and make no mistake about it, I myself had a very large practical side, too. It was so overpowering, in fact, that by the time I was in my second year of university any dream or even desire to pursue a creative life had completely deserted me, not to return until decades later.

The truth was that over the years I had cultivated a kind of picture of what artistic people were like–not like me, of that I was certain. I saw them as free spirits, free to believe things even if they couldn't see hard, scientific proof–something that I did need in my early adulthood. They were much more interesting than I was. Artists had style, flair and passion. I certainly had no flair and had yet to truly find my passion. They had angst in their lives. Where else would that creative tension come from? Any angst in my life was fully suppressed. Indeed, there was ample material in books and movies that a non-artist might come to the conclusion that being happy and having a fulfilling life, or even appearing to, were anathema to the creative process. The truth was that I envied actors, musicians, writers and dancers. I sometimes still fantasized about being an actress, knowing full well that this was far behind me. I would never be a part of that world. Then Gillian called.

Why would any agent want to represent my son? He was still months away from celebrating his fourth birthday. Sure, he was cute and could talk up a storm and he was personable. But was he an actor? Gillian, however, was insistent and I suppose I was intrigued by the idea. Deep down, though, I was horrified that I should pursue this as a kind of vicarious way to reach my own unfulfilled dream. This horror probably pushed me to be a bit overly cautious.

So, Ian and I met with Lara, a local talent agent who as far as I could see was mostly involved in the local fashion industry, if I may use the phrase loosely. The fashion industry in our city revolved largely around fashion shows for local malls during the back-to-school rush, television commercials and fund-raisers for charity. Lara was young and blond and perky, but along with that liveliness I sensed a kind of shrewdness about her. I liked that.

Lara took one look at Ian and said, "I'd like to represent him."

What? How could she possibly have come to that conclusion? I thought. She didn't have any idea of whether or not he could act. How naive I was. That little detail of acting mattered not in the slightest, as I was soon to discover. How he looked had a great deal more to do with his prospects than talent ever would.

"When directors need kids under four or five, they usually use their own kids or friends' kids. But hc's got a great look." Then she looked at me thoughtfully and said, "Do you act?"

I think that for just a split-second my head began to buzz. Was it a trick question for parents? Could I act? Of course I could. I used to act. No, to be truthful I had to admit that I acted every day as I stood in front of all those rapt university students. Every professor was an actor wasn't she?

"I have dozens of young, pretty model-type faces." Lara's voice brought me abruptly back to the present and to the current reality. She placed her hand on a pile of photos on the corner of her desk, "But everyone seems to want thirty- or forty-something women who can look like business women or housewives."

I didn't know whom 'everyone' or the ubiquitous 'they' really were, and I didn't know whether to be flattered or insulted by her offer of representation in light of her comment, but here was my chance. I wallowed for another moment in thoughts of that kind of possibility that comes to us once in a while in life. As we get older, however, we have a better sense of timing, and my inherent sense kicked in. I knew that I was here for Ian, not me. I had a career. I loved my students, performing for them every day, and I was writing books that people published. They weren't novels, but they were real books nonetheless. No, the time was not right, I thought, thanking her and politely turning down her offer. She sighed and took out a standard agent's representation contract and Ian was signed. We left the office and life went on.

I had all but forgotten about that meeting when the telephone rang two months later. "Can you bring Ian to an audition tomorrow at 1:20?" It was Lara. "They're doing a sitcom pilot and are looking for a little boy."

What Lara didn't tell me at the time, and I was too uninitiated to ask, was that the 'they' she was talking about were a local production company and the Canadian Broadcasting Corporation (CBC) and that they had already auditioned over 50 little boys in Toronto. What I did wonder, however, was who would do a sitcom in our little city of Halifax?

I took Ian to the audition that was memorable only for the sheer number and intensity of all the little boys and their anxious mothers. I must admit I felt a bit proud when the casting assistant asked if Ian had an agent and I said, "Yes," although we had no resumé or head shots. Reflecting on my reaction later, I couldn't imagine how I could have been more ridiculous. But at least I had kept it to myself.

After this encounter we again forgot all about it. Then, on a cold November day, Lara called again. She was very excited as she said, "Ian has a callback."

"A what?" I said rather stupidly, I'm afraid. It's very difficult to get excited about something when you haven't a clue about the jargon.

"He's on the short list," she said. "They really liked him."

Short lists I understood, so I asked Ian if he wanted to go to an audition again, to which he enthusiastically answered, "Yes," and I took him to the callback. This I remember better. It was held down town at a local meditation-training hall. We waited on a narrow landing under the stairs that led from the second to the third floor of this old, dark warehouse building. Already there awaiting their turns were about six other little boys and their mothers and six little girls, about three or four years older than the boys, along with their mothers. I tried to get a good look at them as surreptitiously as I could. They all seemed to have a different look about them. One at a time the casting agent called us into the room.

I took Ian by the hand and asked him if he was having fun. He sure was, he told me, smiling. The door was opened for us and we walked into an enormous auditorium-like hall with rows of tall windows on each side. The room was empty except for a single long table at which sat three rather large men. There was a tripod-mounted camera to the side and a small wooden chair all by itself in the middle of the room facing the table. They asked Ian to take a seat by himself in the chair in the middle. It was one of those old-fashioned wooden chairs with high arms and a slatted back that you might see beside a desk in a movie about a 1940s newsroom. There was no cushion. Ian looked at me for approval and I nodded. Off he trotted, climbed up onto the chair and turned to sit eyeball-to-eyeball with LA director, the trench-coat clad Ted Kotcheff, who had recently directed Sylvester Stallone in an action movie. Beside him sat Canadian television legend Louis Del Grande whose show *Seeing Things* had been a CBC staple for years. Louis was the star of this new show. If Ian got the job, he would be playing Louis' little grandson. The third man was the local producer.

I stood back against the wall determined not to be the stereotypical, in-your-face, wannabe stage mom. Ian sat there looking tiny and vulnerable, but smiling at them. They asked him a few questions all of which my verbose little guy answered with one word apiece. Hardly an auspicious sign for an actor, I thought.

"Do you have a grandfather?" Louis asked.

"No," said Ian. In fact he had two; it had evidently slipped his mind that day.

Just then Louis came out from behind the big table. "Would you let me pick you up?" he asked, glancing at me for my approval.

I nodded and Ian did as well. Louis picked him up and said, "How would you like it if I swung you around?"

Ian said that would be okay too.

I watched as something remarkable happened. We often hear about rapport and chemistry, but that afternoon I saw it take form before my eyes. As Louis held Ian in his arms and on his lap, they laughed and talked and the ice was broken. They could have been real-life grandfather and grandson in that moment. Ian shook hands with each one of the towering men on the way out the door and said to me, "That was fun."

Five days later he had the part and I was a stage mom.

THREE

Stage Mother

...stage mother is the term for the mother of a child actor.
The mother will often drive their [sic] child to auditions,
make sure they are on the set on time, etc.
In some cases, the mothers have been known to be
obnoxious by demanding special treatment
for their sons or daughters.
Calling someone a stage mother has therefore
at times been used as a derogatory term for a parent
who thinks that their [sic] child is better than any other
children and therefore should be treated better.

– Wikipedia

Utter the phrase "stage mother" to just about anyone you know and you've begun to conjure in their minds a whole series of images that evoke the stereotypical harridan whose idea of a good day is one in which other people's children are rejected and hers are not. I once read a tongue-in-cheek story on the internet about the Annual Stage Mothers' Awards with award categories that included Best Passive-aggressive Mother and Child Most Likely to Need Ritalin. In fact, most people seem to believe that stage parents in general are either trying to make their children into stars for the money or have secret fantasies about them being discovered and at the very least living vicariously through their offspring. The truth is I've met both kinds.

The mom who wrote the definitive book on meddlesome stage moms had to be the fictitious Mama Rose, mother of Gypsy Rose Lee in the stage musical Gypsy. We could all have learned a thing or two from her as she pushed her daughters toward stardom. But the most interesting term I've ever heard applied to this breed of parent is the 'helicopter parent', that kind of hovering presence who can't seem to get out of the child's way. The term is now widely used to describe parents of college kids, but it seems to fit the stage-mom breed equally as well. They hover about in the faces of all those who have the misfortune to come into contact with their children, believing that they are only doing what's right for their children yet all the while alienating the very people who have power over the kids (...but much more about them later). I was determined not to live up to the standards.

People seem to find the idea of the stage mother endlessly fascinating. Even those other parents who protest that they would never put their children on television often harbour deeply buried envy of what appears to be a glamorous undertaking. But really, who are we kidding? Children heading for auditions are a dime a dozen in North America, and the larger the metropolis in which you live, the bigger the stage-mom industry. In the larger urban centres, most days there are casting calls and how many of those children ever really build careers? Perhaps more to the point: how many of them even want careers as actors? I often wondered how many of the parents we kept running into at auditions hoped that stardom was just around the next corner–the result of just one more audition. The worst part was that I didn't know if I could honestly answer the question myself. It became a regular struggle.

As a stage mom, the truth is that you *have* to be every bit as involved as your child. I didn't really consider this as we signed that first contract. Whether you like it or not, it's a fact of the life. Someone has to field the audition calls, if he's old enough to be in school pick him up from school and explain to the teacher why he's leaving in the middle of the day, drive him downtown, fill in the audition form, hand over the inevitable and required head shots and resumés which you've arranged, paid for and/or written and copied, wait with a bunch of tense not-so-friendly mothers or fathers and their coiffed kids, at least the girls were usually coiffed, drive him back to school and in the end convey the good or bad news.

And then when the news is good…well, the tasks are endless. The truth is, however, I loved it. I loved Ian's obvious delight at landing every role he auditioned for in the first year or two after that fateful phone call from my student. I loved meeting the local television and commercial producers. I loved watching the crews work. I loved that Ian loved it.

That first television experience was an eye-opener for all three of us. Here's what we learned.

First, we learned that we would never ever, no matter how much money we might be offered, let a TV crew use our home for a location shoot. We spent a week driving Ian back and forth to a beautiful home overlooking the mouth of the Halifax harbour. Owned by a well-known and well-heeled businessman and his family, the house was nothing short of spectacular–although seeing it on the screen later didn't really do it justice. It had wonderful spacious rooms with soaring ceilings in the main spaces and a breathtaking view of the rocks and out to sea. The curving staircase swept up three stories and led to even more fabulous ocean vistas. I wondered more than once that week what would possess such a family to allow a crew to tape cables to their carpets, traipse up and down stairs in wet, snow-covered boots, completely re-outfit their dining room and kitchen and clog up the street with trailers, trucks and vans of every description. And what about the neighbours? I can only imagine how they must have felt.

The second lesson we learned was that our little boy had an innate sense of commitment. I'm not sure if this is instinctive in some people or he truly learned it from us; nevertheless, he worked like a trooper, doing as he was asked by the director and treating everyone with a kind of inborn professional presence. It was a pleasure to see and it made us proud. On the fourth day of shooting, he had been there for eight hours and was barely within his union requirements for breaks (I kept a close eye on that), Ian had told me he was so tired. When the director said, "Ian, we need you for just one more take," Ian perked up and faced the camera with the aplomb of a seasoned thespian. Then we took him home and tucked him into bed.

We also learned that no matter what people say about a TV pilot, no matter how positive the newspaper reviews, no matter how large the audience, no matter how much you hope that it might happen, there is no predicting the outcome. When the show was not picked up, we had distinctly mixed feelings. In some ways, after getting to know the participants, we knew that it would be quite a blow to them; still more than that, however, we actually kind of enjoyed the whole thing and it appeared that Ian did as well. I did, however, have a deeply held concern that I had kept to myself. I wasn't at all certain that I wanted my little boy to grow up in front of a television audience as had happened to so many child actors whose regular television gigs went on for years.

We chalked it all up to experience and Ian lived the experience over and over watching the videotape of the show with great delight. Often we could hear him playing with his toy bears and other stuffed animals, giving them specific directions. "We're rolling," he'd intone. "Speed...and action!" It was a new part of his vocabulary.

One fine weekday afternoon when Ian was six years old, we made our way downtown to Filmworks, one of the only two casting companies in the city. We were becoming regulars there and the casting people knew Ian well. He was known as a kid who was easy to direct and well-behaved, two of the most important traits for a child actor. The place was located in the part of town that had been previously ignored but was beginning to experience an urban renaissance–involving everything around except the scruffy tavern next door and the place itself. It was old, grimy and always in a state of complete dishevelment.

The tiny waiting room held several young boys and their moms and we were all there for the same thing: to let our children audition for a television commercial. In an uncharacteristically friendly approach, the mom sitting next to me asked, "Does your son get nervous at these things? My Joey gets so nervous. Today he even threw up in the car on the way over."

I didn't quite know what to say. I was appalled at the thought that a child might be brought to an audition in such a state of anxiety that he would be physically ill. I wanted to ask her why she had brought him, but instead I answered her question.

"No," I said. "I'm not sure Ian even knows what it means to be nervous. Does your son enjoy this?"

"Oh, yes, of course," she said brightly, clearly not quite understanding the thrust of my question. "I'm an actress myself, you know. I get nervous at auditions, too."

She didn't need to say another word. By that time in the unfolding of my career as a stage mom, I had seen enough 'actors' bringing their children to auditions to know that it was often the parents more than the children who really wanted this to happen.

Above all else, the stage mom is a mom. I realized through all this I was learning a lot about being a mom, a lot that would help later. I now realized that my caution about living vicariously through my child was spot-on. I knew that doing so would be a mistake.

We did enjoy Ian's foray into the acting world, but we had to be careful.

FOUR

The Mother of All Arts

*The dance is the mother of the arts. Music and poetry
exist in time; painting and architecture in space.
But the dance lives at once in time and space.*
–Curt Sachs

I have often wondered as I reflected on my own childhood, how much more of it I might 'remember' if we had had the benefit of video back in those days. My own childhood is a blur with but a few major events rising above the haze. I'm part of a generation of parents whose children seem to have perfect recall — yet I think these are constructed memories that are as two-dimensional as the video images that have captured them. And there are few children who have more interesting video moments than those whose appearances graced not only the television sets of their parents, but also those of a region or even a nation. Such are the memories of childhood for a kid whose image used to pop up in commercials while we watched a favourite show.

I particularly remember a set of commercials Ian did at the age of seven for a local car dealership. The advertising agency that hired him was run by a young woman who had her sights set on carving out a career as a high-powered marketer. She was more memorable, however, for her wild hair, the height of her heels and her breathtaking lack of knowledge about writing and producing commercials. But that only made the experience all the more humorous, and Ian had enjoyed himself immensely.

My career as a stage mother, however, also took a foray into theatre. A musician who had paid a few bills during medical school by playing gigs at local hot spots, my husband had settled into his career with a significant avocation as a drummer. He played old rock and roll, jazz, and most importantly from my perspective as a stage mom, musical theatre.

It was late 1993, about six months after Ian had made his debut as a television actor, when the annual Nova Scotia Drama League fund-raiser came along. Art was to be part of the pit band for the musical Annie that was being staged at the Arts Centre of Dalhousie University. He happened to mention Ian's burgeoning acting career to the director who was only too happy to have a cute little boy who was clearly directable join the cast to take a walk-on part. Ian was thrilled and I got to spend lots of time around actors without actually having to put myself front and centre as I had considered in my early years.

On opening night I watched from the wings as my little guy donned his news-boy outfit, complete with tweed pork-pie hat, and made his entrance holding the hand of one of the adult actors. His role was to walk across the stage holding an apple for sale. He even got to be part of a musical number, and although the director didn't really expect him to learn the words, he did. After the final curtain, as Ian and I made our way out to the front of the theatre, people greeted us who seemed to think Ian's performance was particularly notable. Odd, I thought. Then Art, who by this time had made his way out of the orchestra pit, laughingly filled me in.

After the curtain call–Ian's first–when the lights on stage went down and the rest of the cast melted into the darkness of the back of the stage to allow the curtain to close in front of them, there stood Ian stage left and oblivious to the heavy velvet curtain swishing past him, seemingly mesmerized by the applause. A moment or two went by as he remained the only one on the stage still standing in the spotlight, the audience loving it, until one of the girls who had played an orphan returned and took his hand, the two of them receding into the shadow. The next day's newspaper story began by mentioning the adorable little guy who had remained on stage; it was clear people thought it had been planned. The result, however, was that in those few seconds that he stood there alone on the stage basking in the audience's approval, something happened. Ian was hooked.

This stage show became an annual event for Ian and Art. Father and son would go off to rehearsal together much as other little Canadian boys and their fathers might go to the hockey rink in the wee hours of a cold Saturday morning. Each year the show was different and each year he had a larger role. One year he played a royal prince in *The King and I* and even had a line. We were so proud. Then they staged *The Wizard of Oz*.

The munchkin was memorable for a couple of reasons. First, Ian had a cold for the entire run of the show. Mom was reduced to back stage nose blower and I cringed every time he coughed. There's never a good moment.

The show was memorable for one other very important reason. In my career as a stage mom, it was perhaps the most important watershed of my avocation.

"Mom," said seven-year-old Ian a few days after the show had ended, "I'd like to learn more about dancing."

Dancing? Wow, those were not words that I ever anticipated hearing from a child of mine, whether a son or a daughter. Indeed Art never expected to hear them either. I had never taken a dance class in all my 42 years and I had certainly never wanted to be a ballerina –a dream we're often led to believe is the universal desire of young women everywhere. The very idea of wearing a tutu made my hair stand on end.

"Okay," I said carefully. "What kind of dancing would you like to learn about?"

"You know," he said, his eyes widening with remembered delight. "That kind of dancing I did in *The Wizard of Oz*."

I nodded. Other years the production had been fun, with the singing and just being there on stage with the audience in thrall. This year there had been dancing. This year had been special–at least that's how Ian saw it from his seven-year-old's star-struck view.

"I'll see if I can find you a class," I said, not really knowing where one began to search for an appropriate dance class for a little boy in a city like Halifax. To my limited knowledge at the time, Halifax didn't even have the audience interest to support a professional dance troupe of any kind, never mind a ballet company.

Christmas came and went with its usual excitement of a family with a young child and visiting grandparents. When the last ornament had been hauled off to the attic for another year, I sat myself in my office and pulled out the yellow pages.

Dance schools–there were lots of them, it seemed, even in a city that didn't seem to be a big dance town. I ran my finger down the list, quickly scanning for their locations and trying to remember if I had ever heard anything about any of them. I ran my eyes up the list again and they rested on the one name I recognized. I really didn't know anything about this school; I only knew that it rang a bell– albeit the tinkling was faint. So I dialled the number unsure of even what to ask. As I recited my story to the long-suffering woman on the other end of the line, I began to consider my lack of knowledge and a certain discomfiture in this new venture. I hated not being in the know. It was one thing to be a stage mom, but the dance world was really foreign.

After some discussion, together we discovered that the school offered what seemed like the perfect class for a young song and dance man–Song and Dance it was appropriately enough named. That should give him a taste of musical theatre dance, I thought. I parted with my VISA number. Just that easily and unexpectedly I had become a dance mom–not a hockey mom or a soccer mom but a dance mom.

The following Saturday morning Art and I drove Ian down town to take his first class. As with the stage mom experience, I was wholly unprepared for the world I was entering. It was unfamiliar, strange like an alternate universe that existed in parallel with the one I and my family inhabited and felt comfortable in. Art was equally, if not more, out of his depth. Although his now-grown daughter had taken dance classes as a child, it had never been his responsibility to be a part of it–nor had he ever considered a son's entering that world. His older son, my stepson who was by then 27 years old, had played hockey because like every other red-blooded Canadian boy, it's what you did. But here we were entering a dance school as the snow flurries swirled in and around our heads.

Located in a converted brewery on the waterfront, the dance school's building was a little taste of history with original stone walls and tall windows. It had a kind of sturdy look about it, as if it could withstand anything.

We trudged up the three flights of stairs, on every landing pausing just long enough to observe studios populated by every manner of little girl dressed in black tights, pink tights, sweatshirts, T-shirts, ballet slippers, tap shoes. There wasn't a boy in sight. When we emerged at the top of the stairs, we were in the reception area that doubled as a waiting room for parents and students who had arrived early for class and for those parents who waited the entire time their kids were there. Immediately I was in the midst of a swarm of yet more little girls in pink leotards, many clinging to their mothers. Some were even wearing little puffs of pink tulle around their tiny (and some rather ample) waists. I thought I might just suffocate. (Oh, I had a lot to learn.) This was my initiation into what I would eventually refer to as the pink-tutu set.

They were everywhere, those little girls. I began to think about that scene in *Annie* when Miss Hannigan swigs ferociously from her gin bottle all the while singing about little girls. Yes, they were everywhere and it would only get worse.

Undaunted, Ian looked up at me. "Where do I go, Mom?"

We looked around and found the boy's change room, populated that morning by several fathers helping their tiny daughters into pink ballet slippers. Ian was seven and he didn't mind this in the slightest. Not yet, anyway.

Clad in sweat pants and a T-shirt, his usual attire, Ian took his first class that day–Ian and four little girls. That was January and every Saturday morning all through the winter and spring Art and I deposited him in this place. He didn't miss a class.

Five months later, on a beautiful evening late in June, we found ourselves sitting in the Rebecca Cohn auditorium in the Arts Centre on the campus of Dalhousie University across the city from the dance school. The lights were dimmed and the show was about to begin. The thousand-plus seats were filled. Filled! I could hardly believe it. How could this many people be coming to see their children dance? As I looked around at the parents, sisters, squirming brothers, grandparents, aunts and uncles, it came as a shock that it had never even occurred to me to invite Ian's grandparents. This was obviously a bigger deal than I could ever have imagined. Little did I know just how big a deal it was.

Another surprise was just how big this dance school actually was. As the individual classes of students took to the stage, their sheer numbers left me dumbfounded. I had no idea that there were so many packed into those classes. In fact, it had never occurred to me that so many even studied dance in this city.

One after the other the class groups came out on stage to perform. There were the really cute little ones being led on stage by their teachers; there were the jazzy numbers, the tap numbers. Most painful of all were the ballet performances by the older girls who were no longer cute and clearly not headed for careers as professional dancers. In all of this, there were literally hundreds of girls, and fewer than a half dozen boys.

I whispered to Art in the dark, "Well, what do you think? Do you think we've got a dancer on our hands?"

He leaned over and said, "Wait until I've seen him dance." My husband is a very astute man. I guess thirty years as a family doctor had taught him a thing or two.

The moment finally came when the five little song-and-dancers made their way on to the stage. The music was from the musical version of *Anne of Green Gables,* and, although I thought that Ian was taking a song and dance class, they didn't appear to sing; or at least no one could hear them over the sound track. Like Milli Vanilli, they seemed to be lip-synching through the piece as they made their choreographed way around the stage holding over-sized ice cream cone props in front of their faces. The dancing they did that evening didn't really display much in the way of dance steps, or that's the way I saw it with my untrained eye, and yet we could not keep our eyes off our son. His self-assurance and ease with what he was doing was clear: he was the only child who never once glanced at another dancer to check his steps. In those brief moments his innate sense of musicality was so clear.

As I watched from the darkness of the audience, I remembered the violin teacher some four or five years earlier who had told me she thought he was musically gifted. His complete focus now made it look as if he thought he might be the only one on that stage. Two minutes later it was all just a memory. I looked over at Art who had the bewildered look of a man who's just witnessed something completely unexpected. "My God," he said "he's a dancer."

From Art's lips to God's ear–and how God must have laughed! This was no surprise to God.

FIVE

Pink Tights and Tutus

It is rare that one can see in a little boy the promise of a man,
but one can almost always see in a little girl the threat of a woman.
–Alexandre Dumas

I grew up in a family of all girls. An army officer by trade, my beleaguered father dutifully portered us from house to house and army base to army base for all of my childhood. And not one of those base houses had more than one bathroom. For a blissful two years while he worked in an office that was not located on an army base we lived in a civilian house my parents had been forced to buy, and it had two bathrooms. Since I was not yet a teenager then, however, I probably didn't feel the full positive effects of it. When I finally did reach those teen-aged years, I can remember standing outside the bathroom door on more occasions than I actually care to remember, pounding on it in a vain attempt to dislodge one or the other of my sisters. This was a regular occurrence in our home. Over the years since then, I've often thought that this whole experience of being in a household largely of women–and the middle daughter on top of it all–had a profound effect on my attitude toward girls and women and on my relationships with them as I grew up.

This is not to say that I never liked little girls. In fact, at the age of 30 before I met the love of my life, I was living an agreeable life as a single when my younger sister produced the first grandchild of the family. It was yet another girl (my poor father must have thought that he could never get away from it) and my sister asked me to be godmother to little Lesley. I was delighted and happily considered how I might make the best effort in those duties and provide my niece with a glimpse of life outside her mother's realm of control. When I could be cajoled into babysitting even in her very earliest years, Lesley–anywhere between eight months and two years of age–could be found with me on the couch at all hours of the night, happily playing and watching television when her parents came home. I saw no real point in putting her to bed when she didn't really want to go. (This I would get over when I became a parent.) To this day, my sister will often say to Lesley–now a wonderful young woman in her twenties–"You're just like your aunt!" This is not necessarily meant as a compliment.

Throughout my career, I preferred the company of men. I always found them to be more straightforward and honest in confrontational situations, and you could count on them not to run crying from the room in the middle of a meeting. Although I've seen less of this in recent years–perhaps we are progressing as a species, we women–I was the flabbergasted witness to such an outburst in professional situations on more than one occasion. I've always been just a little uncomfortable around so many women.

You can imagine my reaction, though, when several months after Ian's birth, my mother said, "Well, if you're going to have only one child, it's best it's a boy."

I could not have agreed more, but on deeper consideration of her remark I had to wonder where this was coming from, from a woman who had three daughters and no sons. The truth is, and will remain, that I'm forever grateful that my only child is a son. Even that happenstance didn't get me off the hook when it came to facing one of my foibles.

Just thinking about it sets my teeth on edge and I can feel the hairs on the back of my neck begin to rise ominously. All those little girls! The dance school was full of them, and all in packs, and worse–their mothers! It was a pink world, this world of dance in general and eventually ballet in particular. The subtle prejudices against boys in dance were many and grew especially galling as it became increasingly clear that Ian was a more talented and passionate dancer than the girls–almost to a person.

Ballet was not even on the radar screen when we put our little son into dance classes. And evidently it wasn't on his either. The autumn after his debut as a dancer, I called the dance school once again to register him for classes. What kind of class did I want? they asked.

I told them that Ian wanted to develop skills in musical theatre dance and I was promptly told that for that he would have to study ballet. When I conveyed this piece of news to Ian, he turned up his nose.

"Ballet?" he said snorting derisively. "I want to be on Broadway. Why do I have to learn ballet?"

What did I possibly know to provide an answer to this seemingly reasonable question? I did remember seeing *A Chorus Line* some years earlier and recalled the scene where the director who is running the audition stops a young man in the middle of a dance routine. He asks him where he trained in dance. The young man hesitates and mentions a few dance classes. The director asks if he has studied ballet. The young man says no. The director then indicates to him that he is not to dance. When the young man continues with the exercise, the director becomes agitated. He clearly does not want to see any dancers who are not properly trained in ballet. Or at least that's how I remember the scene. So, I used this information to try to suggest to Ian that if he really wanted to be a Broadway dancer, he would have to bite the bullet and study ballet but it would be his decision. We suggested to him that he also take jazz classes and he agreed.

So began another session of classes and so began my eye-opening experience of being not only a dance mom in general, but a ballet mom in particular.

There were two other boys in Ian's very large ballet class and four others in his jazz class. They were the only boys in this large school. Of the two boys in ballet, one was there clearly under duress from a mother who was determined her son should have this experience, and the other one had been weaned in a dance studio: his mother was one of the school instructors. He did, however, demonstrate little interest in ballet and even less talent. I quickly learned, and just from casual observation, that a lack of musicality was a serious obstacle to success in dance of any kind. What this kid lacked in that department, though, Ian made up for in spades.

But the class was so big! Moreover the instructor, I discovered, was a seventeen-year-old student of the school's advanced program who had even less of an idea as to how to control a large group of children than I did. She was energetic and seemed always to be smiling, even if it was through gritted teeth when she found the boys' level of energy just a bit too much. She had a long way to go in learning how to help them refocus. Near the end of the class, just to see what was going on, sometimes I would hover outside the door with the other ballet mothers and the odd ballet dad.

The studio was a swarm of bodies; it was so overcrowded to my eye. But then, what did I know about ballet classes? I knew very little, so I chose to keep quiet and just observe. I thought that I might actually learn something. At the very least I recognized my own limitations.

The subtle prejudices against the boys at this school began to emerge in small ways. First, there was that sign on the girls' washroom giving very clear direction that no male presence should ever cross the threshold. God forbid that a little boy might come upon a girl forcing her ample bottom into a tight leotard. No such protection of privacy held for the boys, however. Every Saturday morning you could find three, four or even five little girls in the boys' change room with their dads who had clearly been assigned dance supervision duties that week. I bristled at the thought that it was acceptable for the girls to be in the boys' change room but never the other way around. When Ian finally did begin to notice this apparent unfairness, I suggested that he simply strip off some morning. "That ought to send the little girls permanently flying out the door,"I thought. He laughed, recognizing his mother's odd sense of humour, but in his nine-year-old wisdom even then he recognized this as one of his mother's idiosyncracies.

In January of that year, at the beginning of the winter term, I found myself standing outside the boys' change room one Saturday morning. Art was out driving around trying to find a place to park while I wondered just what took our young son so long to change. I was soon being entertained, though, by the mothers who had lined up at the desk that was about six feet away from the boys' change room door. They were registering their daughters for classes for the term. I didn't even bother trying not to eavesdrop.

"I'd like my daughter in that class," says the mother across the desk from the receptionist as she points to a class on the list.

"Okay." The receptionist pulls a registration form from the corner of the desk. "How will you be paying?"

"Are there any boys in that class?" says the mother, completely oblivious to anyone who might be listening.

"Boys? What do you mean?"

"Are there any boys in that class?" repeats Mom. "I don't want my daughter in a class with boys. I find they're too disruptive."

"Disruptive?" I thought. I had to physically prevent myself from taking the two steps to get close enough to slap her. I stood there fuming but said nothing.

When I thought about the incident later, I wondered if she had even considered who those female dancers would be dancing with all those years later. Since there were really no other mothers of boys that I could ever identify and talk to, I began to wonder if it was just me. Did I have some kind of a problem with the hordes of little girls so that I projected upon them and their mothers this perceived attitude? I couldn't be sure.

On one of those early January mornings, Ian came down to the car waving a piece of paper. "They gave this to me today," he said. "I'm supposed to give it to you."

It was a brochure about a newly-formed ballet class for boys. One of the local teachers, an experienced woman from another dance school in the city, had recognized that the boys were lost among

43

the hordes of girls. If they were to keep boys in dance and even encourage more to follow their interest in music and movement, they needed to be able to find one another. She also thought it would be useful if they came together once a month under the tutelage of a male ballet teacher. Evidently there are aspects of training boys that differ from girls' training. *Quelle surprise!*

When we asked Ian if he'd like to attend, he said, "Yes," but that he still liked his jazz classes better than his ballet classes. So we added another class to our monthly inventory of activities and we took him to this class for boys. As much as it might have been a revelation for Ian to be dancing with other boys who shared his interest, it was perhaps even more of a revelation for me. I finally met another mother of a boy who truly loved to dance and was talented as well.

She was a wonderfully confident woman, a specialist physician by background, who headed one of the departments at the medical school. She and her husband, also a physician, and their children had recently relocated from Winnipeg where her dance-mad son had been taking recreational classes with the school associated with the Royal Winnipeg Ballet. She was not terribly impressed with the ballet world for boys in our fair city, an opinion I could hardly dispute. We chatted after class one day and I discovered that I was indeed not alone in my observation that the dance school where we had taken Ian initially was in many ways not the place for a boy. She told us about a place called the Maritime Conservatory of Performing Arts where the dance classes were small and where the teacher who had developed the class for boys headed the dance department. We wondered if it might not be time to take action and find another school.

Our inclination to take this action was solidified as the June performance approached again. As the school began publicity for this performance, it was clear that there was little consideration of the boys. They tried to get the entire student body to purchase T-shirts with the annual logo and theme emblazoned across the front. The theme that year was "Dancing through the Pages," and each of the class performances was to be based on a book or famous story. Splashed across the front of this T-shirt was a dancer on her toes with a long skirt flowing around her legs.

"I'm not wearing one of those!" Ian said. "It's for girls."

An astute observation, we thought.

On the night of the performance, Ian's ballet class of three boys and fifteen girls danced the story of Madeleine, the French story of little girls who attended a Parisian school. It was difficult to tell but it seemed that the boys simply played girls although in fairness, they didn't have to wear the same costumes as the girls. As Art and I discussed this afterwards, we wondered why the teacher couldn't have found a story that had both girls and boys as characters. Surely it wouldn't have been such a stretch. Nevertheless, Ian did enjoy the performance, even if he too recognized that the story had no boys in it.

As we made our way backstage to find our boy and take him home that evening, we crossed paths with one of the senior teachers at the school.

"You know," she said, "Ian's headed for the National Ballet School." Then she waved and continued walking toward the other side of the stage.

What exactly was she trying to say? It was a kind of throw-away remark, and yet it seemed strange. It was clear that the school recognized Ian had innate talent, but there was no follow-up. What does a parent confronted with this kind of news make of it? We did what any concerned parents would do: we pulled him out of that school and enrolled him in the Conservatory. By that time, the one other boy studying at the Conservatory whose mother I had met at the boys' ballet class had already been accepted to the summer program at the National Ballet School. Perhaps they knew something that Ian's current school was clearly missing.

SIX

Changing Perspectives

If we don't change, we don't grow.
If we don't grow, we aren't really living.
–Gail Sheehy

Through the years Art had often found it useful to remind me of that quote from Heraclitus: "Nothing endures but change." And so it goes. Life evolves and everything has a beginning, a middle and an end.

That spring when Ian debuted as a dancer, a lot of important changes happened in our lives. The previous autumn we had been seized by the notion that we were ready to move out of the city to somewhere a bit more idyllic. We had sold our original condo and bought our city house in an up-and-coming, slightly more suburban neighbourhood about two months before Ian was born. It was a wonderful Cape Cod with all the dream requirements for a house with a baby who would soon grow to be a toddler, a pre-schooler and eventually a grade-schooler. The house boasted large, formal living spaces that one would never need to enter unless compelled to do so by visiting relatives or friends. Even more appealing was its huge main-floor family room with vaulted ceilings and a cosy fireplace just off the kitchen, so a mom or dad could cook while at the same time keeping a close eye on the offspring, and it was close to a school. As he grew, Ian especially loved the enormous basement play room where toys and other large kid paraphernalia could be out of sight except when being used, and Art loved the sound-proofed music room where his rock band could rehearse without disturbing the upstairs ambience. He and four other doctors convened for weekly practice and did charity gigs.

We loved that house and never considered moving, but things change.

After almost eight years of enjoying our home and neighbourhood, the area was growing. We no longer had the clear view of the park across the street since they had built a very large house on the lot; the wandering deer had been replaced by children playing noisy street hockey outside my office window in the front of the house, and we were tired of driving an hour-and-a-half every weekend to our lakefront cottage. A Newfoundlander by birth, Art missed the salt water so we decided that we wanted to be beside the water all the time, not just on weekends, and we embarked on a search for ocean frontage.

On a snowy Boxing Day that winter, our real estate agent called in a panic. "You have to see this house and it won't be on the market long."

To paraphrase Caesar, we went, we saw, we loved–and we bought. That of course meant that we had two properties we had to sell. It took three months of constant vacuuming, general primping and disappearing for viewings; we finally sold the city house. The cottage took a few months longer (who wants to slog through the snow to see a lakefront cottage in the middle of winter?), but the first offer was very close to what we had asked and we snatched it up so we could get on with our lives.

That spring when we weren't conveying Ian from one dance class to another, we were driving to and from movie shoots. The now well-known director Thom Fitzgerald had cast Ian in his first film *The Hanging Garden*. It was an odd script, but it was an experience we couldn't deny Ian. There were several days of location shooting outside Halifax and another week or so at a makeshift sound studio in a nearby industrial park. One or the other of us had to be on set at all times with him because of his age. Although it was time-consuming, we actually quite enjoyed hovering on the periphery of these creative individuals, a role that would become very familiar to us over the next few years. It was an interesting process and when the film debuted at the local film festival and then went on to win awards at the Toronto International Film Festival, we were proud to have been even a small, tangential part of it. Thom, the director, has gone on to make a number of successful movies with Hollywood casts. Occasionally Ian receives a check for residuals. It's still a fond memory. But all of that happened as we readied ourselves to move. In the background add a new puppy (what had we been thinking!) who had wiggled his way into our hearts and home the spring before.

Finally, the move was set for mid-May. One week before we were to take possession of our new oceanfront home, a phone call from Art's father changed our preparations. Art's 80-year-old mom had been rushed to the hospital and the outlook was not good. An only child, he (and I) knew what he had to do. He called me from his office mid-afternoon and by the time he arrived home, I had him booked on an evening flight to St. John's. That was Thursday.

Within thirty-six hours she had died with her only son by her side. When Art called, I thought about my only son and wondered how many years we would have to enjoy each other's company. I spent the next several days in Newfoundland with Art who then stayed behind to help his father, a man who had never dreamed that he'd be the one left behind. I had to be home to meet the packers who were coming the next Thursday.

They finally arrived. I'm sure the first thing out of my mouth that morning was, "Please be sure to close the door behind you each time you come in or out so that the dog doesn't get out."

Gambit was now a year old, a feisty little fox terrier who had wangled himself firmly into our lives. He would not listen to me: I'm told that terriers are difficult to train because, from their perspective, they do something only when there is an obvious a reason for it. Following the commands of one person in the household—in this case that person was Art—was all he could muster.

Art had flown back from The Rock earlier that day and had taken one look at the mess and fled to his office to catch up on patient reports and other mail. I heard the terrified yelp from somewhere outside the house and in a moment I knew. They had let him out. Sure enough, I ran outside to find the two packers in their truck eating their five o'clock sandwiches. "Did you see the dog?" I asked, terrified of what might have happened.

"Oh, yeah," says one of them. "He ran out when we left the house."

Had it occurred to them to tell someone? I hadn't the time to follow-up on that thought, but would return to it later. To say the least, I was livid–and frightened. It turned out I had good reason to be frightened.

By then a car driven by a terrified and terribly concerned young woman had already hit Gambit. One broken jaw and three days of veterinary care later we had moved into our new home on the shores of beautiful St. Margaret's Bay, a thirty-five-minute commute from downtown but a world away from any city.

That move proved to be pivotal in Ian's education. Products of the public school system ourselves, we had never seriously considered putting Ian in private schools although it seemed *de rigeur* for most of our acquaintances and colleagues. To continue with our previous perspective, we registered Ian at the local public school and that September I left the eight-year-old standing on a rural highway to await a school bus as I motored on to the city to teach. Leaving him waiting for the school bus was one of the hardest things I ever had to do. I wanted to wait and follow it to the school, just to see that he got there. But I knew that was foolish and I had a gaggle of students at the university awaiting my wisdom in a class at nine. What an experience that was for a mother! That was only the beginning of a strange year.

One thing that we could always say we had done for our son was to make him flexible and adaptable. This was to stand him in very good stead in the years to come. That year I tried to be adaptable myself and decided to take a more active part in the life of the school, joining for the first time the Parent/Teacher Group. As an adult I had never been a joiner and the groupthink mentality had always been a problem for me–perplexing at its most benign and anger-producing at its most malignant.

About six months into that first year, Ian came home one day excited that the school would be putting on a play, *Jack and the Beanstalk*. He, of course, would audition for the part of Jack. He seemed a shoe-in from what I had seen of his classmates. His interest and experience in acting seemed to far surpass that of anyone he knew.

The day of the audition finally came.

"How did it go?" I asked when he returned from school that day. I expected an excited response to the prospect of getting on stage again.

"Okay," he said slowly. "The teacher who's directing the play took me aside after the audition and told me that I was the best one."

This was promising.

Then he continued. "But he told me that he wasn't going to cast me as Jack so that he could give someone else the chance since I had experience."

What? I was immediately furious with the kind of righteous indignation a mother feels for a child wronged. I was well over forty by that time and had had my own experience of injustice in work situations, so I chose my words carefully. Just say the word, I thought, and I'll be down their throats.

"How do you feel about that?" I said.

"It's okay, Mom. It would be good for the other guy who gets to play it. I'm going to be the one who sells Jack the magic beans." It was a much smaller role.

Possessing great generosity of spirit is how many of Ian's teachers in future would describe him. This was the first inkling I had that perhaps my little boy was more mature even than I was; perhaps wise beyond his years. That didn't stop me, though, from considering the injustice of it all.

I thought about what our schools were like when it came to sports, for example. Hockey naturally came to mind in a country full of hockey-mad kids and adults. I wondered what would happen if such a decision was made about the hockey team. How would mom and dad respond to the star hockey player being benched during a game to let all the others have more ice time? The way schools think about competitive hockey would mean that the best player would never be subjected to such treatment, especially if it meant the difference between winning and losing.

It was a watershed moment for me that struck like a bolt of lightning. The arts were in serious trouble in our school system, threatened at every turn–by fiscal restraints, by thoughtlessness, by a lack of understanding about what they contribute both to our economy and our souls. This realization would lead me to change the focus of my own community service from health-related causes to the performing arts. When the Director of the Maritime Conservatory of Performing Arts approached me later that year to sit on the Board of Governors, I didn't hesitate. The decision also led to an opening of different educational opportunities for Ian but not before I, as a mother, had some sense of just desserts.

The night of the play arrived. Ian had spent days perfecting his few lines and ensuring that his dramatic costume helped him to make an entrance. He might have had only a few lines, but he was taking them seriously. He was so serious about the whole performance that the teacher had asked him to assist with the curtain when he wasn't on stage. I sewed his costume that consisted largely of an enormous black cape that he could swish about menacingly as he told Jack about the magic contained in the beans and admonished him to be careful.

The makeshift auditorium with its equally makeshift stage was full that evening. I had largely gotten over my issue and just looked forward to wishing all the kids well. Ian was magnificent, receiving appreciative applause for his performance. Not much more positive could be said, however, about the rest of the production.

The director/teacher was clearly distraught that evening as he had to repeatedly hiss lines from the sidelines to his Jack who plainly hadn't taken the time or interest to learn them. It would have been embarrassing if it hadn't been so avoidable–and ever so funny. (But I didn't tell anyone that.) He made a point of coming to see us after the show to tell us how well Ian did and to thank him for helping out backstage, to use the term loosely. Did I catch a hint of wistfulness in his voice as he told me how seriously Ian had taken his part and how he had helped him to cajole the others into being more serious? We were happy parents; if perhaps a bit smug as well. It was crystal clear that any school which would treat a performance that way was not the place for Ian.

One Sunday afternoon as we sat outside the studio downtown waiting for Ian after one of the boys' ballet classes, I began to rifle through the brochures that had been placed on the table in the hope that bored parents would do exactly what I was doing. I noticed a brochure for a small private school in the city. "Genuine delight in learning" was its motto and the brochure referred to the curriculum as being arts-based and nurturing the individual student. I took the brochure and passed it to Ian in the car on the way home. Later that evening he emerged from his room. "I'd like to visit this school," he said. So we put the wheels in motion.

It was called The Shambhala Elementary School. On a bright spring day, I took Ian out of his school to spend a day at the newly discovered Shambhala School. The classroom where he spent the day was enormous, with desks on one side and a very large table occupying the other. There was a large basket of recorders, each in its own little handknit sleeve that, I later learned, the students had created themselves. These little sleeves for all the world resembled large, knitted condoms. It seemed that every little Grade 3 student in the school (all eight of them) knew how to knit. Ian would have to get up to speed. It was not a skill that I had shared with my young son. We would also discover that the recorders were a very important part of the fundamental music program at the school. Musically inclined or not, every student learned to play the recorder. Oh, and there was a rocking chair surrounded by large cushions on the floor, no doubt for reading together?

As it happened the school was renting space from the Maritime Conservatory where Ian took his dance classes, a bonus in terms of accessibility from a mom's point of view. I left him in the apparently capable hands of the teacher who was also the co-founder and headmistress of the school that housed only Grade Primary to Grade six.

At the end of the day Ian was smitten. The other students had welcomed him warmly into their little group and it appeared that the defining feature of the experience was the lunch procedures, which he excitedly described to me. The students and their teacher all sat around that table on the non-desk side of the classroom and took out their lunches. Before they could eat, though, there was a very important ritual. They had to light a candle, just as we usually did at home in the evening. (Although I admit it was not quite a ritual in our home; rather I lit it when I set the table. I just happened to like candles.) One child each day had the privilege of striking the match and then lighting it. Ian was looking forward to his turn.

That day marked the beginning of a long and often odd relationship between me, as a parent, and the Shambhala school community in Halifax. The school was non-sectarian, although established by the local Buddhist community who had largely immigrated to Halifax from Boulder, Colorado, some years ago. Its approaches, however, derived from the peaceful, loving-kindness philosophy of the Shambhala tradition. I could not have been more pleased that Ian had found this place.

He completed his year in the school where he had started, and then we all bid farewell to the public school system. Now that the academics had been looked after and he was safely ensconced in dance classes at the Maritime Conservatory, we could breathe a sigh of relief and get on with things. With the mentor we had found, this was so much easier.

SEVEN

The Education of a Ballet Mom

Teachers open the door, but you must enter by yourself.
–Chinese Proverb

I don't truly understand why people dance, and for most of my life I understood very little about dance in general or ballet in particular. Although I thought could tell the difference between ballet and jazz, what was the difference between jazz and modern dance? I know now that there's a considerable difference–in fact they're not the same at all, but I didn't know it at the beginning of my foray into the world of being a ballet mom. I certainly did not know what a *fouetté* was nor could I tell you when someone was doing a *tendu*. And what about a *glissade*? Not a clue. The truth is, though, I'm still not sure you really need to know these things to appreciate and enjoy dance as an audience member. Yet I certainly thought it would be helpful and fun to learn more about the language of dance. At least then I could understand my son's jargon! But the motivation for dance was and continues to be quite a different thing for me.

I don't know why some people want to dance. I don't know why my son *must* dance; I only know that he *must* and I know this not because I have some kind of mother's intuition–rather I know it because he told me. This has been an important lesson from my child and I have found that it is always in my best interest to listen. I did not, however, understand at the beginning that for most dancers this is true as well. It has become clear to me that dancers in general and ballet dancers in particular dance because they have no choice. It's a part of who they are. That's the difference between them and the rest of us. It is this compulsion to dance to music that

55

few others can hear. I still struggle to understand the origin of this compulsion and how it must feel to want to move to music in front of an audience. Somewhere between that first moment I knew that I was a ballet mom and these many years later, I learned a lot and came to appreciate what it gives to us–to our souls. It was not a smooth process nor was it a clear path.

A few years before I even considered the possibility that I might ever be a mother, when I was almost thirty years old, I saw my first ballet. During my childhood, ballet was as far off my parents' radar as anything could have been, so I knew nothing whatsoever about it. I was always a fan of classical music–perhaps it was a vestige of those shudder-inducing piano classes and the hours of unwelcome practice–but I had never put music and movement together in that way. For me, as a young adult in the 1980s, moving to music took place strictly on the dance floor of a discotheque! So when I finally did see my first ballet, I really didn't know quite what to make of it. In any case, the fact that I was even there that day was something unintended. Unlike many who are moved and inspired by their first experience of watching a ballet, I was nonplussed–indeed, I have to admit I wasn't really that impressed.

It was the middle of the 1980s when I, like everyone else I knew, was decked out in line-backer shoulder pads and Simon Chang suits by day and tights and leg warmers by night. (OK, I never really wore them outside my apartment, but I did own a pair.). I was dating a man who had occasion to move to Australia for a two-year stint and he asked me to take a trip over for a few weeks. It was during that sojourn in Sydney that I saw my first ballet.

We'd gone to the ballet only because it happened to be on offer at the Sydney Opera House. Moreover, we wanted to experience the setting. What's a trip down under without a visit to the famed opera house? Since we were both classical music fans anyway, and ballet had the added value of visual interest, we went. On the bill that evening was *Romeo and Juliet* and I loved Prokofiev's music, but I seem to remember more about the music than the dancing. Perhaps that's because about a half hour into the show, I concluded that ballet consisted of about ten or fifteen different moves all strung together in different combinations. Since we were too far away from the stage, practically suffering nosebleeds from the thin air, for me to see faces or gluteal muscles under the men's tights, I decided I might as well just close my eyes and enjoy the music. So I did, I'm now embarrassed to say. My companion that evening was of little help either. As I recall he was indifferent to the ballet, taking more of an interest in the architecture than the event itself. That was the last time I even thought about ballet until the teacher at Ian's dance school said he'd have to take ballet classes.

Neither of us knew a *jeté* from a *pirouette* and it would be many years before I understood what *attitude* meant. To most parents of teenagers it would come to mean one thing, but for us it was very different. I knew that if I were going to understand and enjoy my only child's pursuit, I'd have to educate myself. So too would the dad who freely admitted that had this happened twenty years earlier in his life, he would probably have just responded to the dance plea by helping Ian to lace his skates and learn to take slap shots.

As I've mentioned, I've long believed that you can learn a lot from a good book. With that in mind, I knew I'd have to find one. The problem was, Amazon was still largely in its infancy and there was still a lot of public concern about using a credit card on-line. So, it was back to my roots. My first part-time job in high school and second one in my first year of university had both been working in libraries. Libraries were places that I knew my way around. And then there were the bookstores. During my early years as a mom I was co-authoring books about health care issues with Art, and we were doing book tours and speaking engagements. Often we found ourselves in Toronto where the World's Biggest Bookstore was one of our favourite haunts. I could lose myself in there for hours and so I did, hunting for reference material for budding ballet moms and dads or even more generic dance-parent books. Alas I emerged with...very little. There was next to nothing written specifically for parents of ballet dancers. I'd have to enlarge my search to more general works about ballet–perhaps a memoir or two. I didn't feel the necessity to study the texts about the actual steps themselves. I would leave the details to Ian and his teachers since it was, after all, his life.

What exactly did I learn about ballet in the early years? There was that one book that I devoured for it was the only one of its kind that I could find: *The Parents' Book of Ballet* by Angela Whitehill and William Noble. God love them for taking on the task for what publishers clearly considered a black hole for sales, or there would be more on the subject. It was a sensible book, covering the parenting of ballet kids in a chronological way–what to consider at ages four to seven, eight to twelve and so on. One chapter I found especially poignant, Special Training for Boys. It was brief at only about three or four pages, but at least they acknowledged that boys were, indeed, different. It was all I needed to get started. And when books fail to fill the knowledge gap, you look to a teacher. Luckily for me, the woman who had led us to the best school for Ian became his mentor–and mine as well.

Her name was Barbara Dearborn and she was as unlike the stereotypical ballet teacher as one could find. Serious and well schooled, she was also warm, compassionate and understanding with an undercurrent of disciplined expectation to which Ian responded well. She insisted that her classes be kept small, both for her own teaching and that of the other teachers whose work she supervised. She also insisted that her teachers be well qualified. Unlike Ian's previous school that had used senior students to teach the lower levels of ballet, Barbara's teachers–even those who taught creative movement to three-year-olds–were all qualified dance teachers. I hadn't realized how important this was. Ian loved it and so did I. We also loved the atmosphere of the school, an eclectic mix of dance, instrumental music and voice teachers and students. When Ian was a bit older and studying both voice and ballet, I remember one of his classmates characterizing the school as "…our own little Juilliard." Perhaps a bit of an overstatement, but the sentiment did capture the feel of the school dedicated to an eclectic collection of the performing arts.

Barb had a special understanding that boys were different and needed a different kind of guidance from the girls. It was Barb who sent a video tape and a note to Art and me via Ian. The note suggested that we might be interested in viewing this video about men in ballet and then give her feedback as to whether or not we thought it would be okay for her to show it to Ian. Although I never did meet him in person, that video introduced me to another teacher whom I would find very important in my education as a ballet mom. That teacher was Frank Augustyn, former principal dancer with the National Ballet of Canada and prima ballerina Karen Kain's partner for seven years. But I digress. The video in question...

The video was an episode from a television series called *Footnotes: The Classics of Ballet* that Frank Augustyn hosted for Canadian television in the 1990s. The very first thing I learned from it, despite the focus on ballerinas, tutus and all things pink (at least in my mind) was that ballet for all its grace, delicacy and elegance was not in fact a women's art form. Its historical roots placed it firmly within the male purview, having been created in the court of Louis XIV—*for men.*

What a revelation! So, what happened? It seems that the pointe shoe happened and for some years during the 20th century, men became little more than porters for the women. According to Augustyn, Danish dancer Auguste Bournonville decided this didn't sit well with him, and he vowed to put men back where they belonged in the art form–at the top, or at least centre stage. I liked this Bournonville. It seemed to me, even at this early stage in my development as a ballet mom, that I might have to take on the cause myself. At least I considered it from time to time when I saw that the boys weren't being given their due.

As Art and I watched this video, I began to wonder what Barb thought we ought to see before showing it to Ian. Surely this would be wonderful for him. It was the frank discussion of the perceived effeminate nature of ballet that probably led her to believe that we ought to give her the green light. We didn't have a problem with this at all. However, we did understand that not all parents would be so comfortable with it. Ian had to learn it sooner or later, and the year before he had been called 'ballet boy' by one of his public school classmates, and not as a compliment. When I had asked him how he felt about that remark, he had shrugged and said he just wouldn't talk about it any more.

Probably the most important concrete piece of information I gleaned from the show was the answer to the question that Frank Augustyn said people often asked: What exactly do male ballet dancers wear under those tights?

To be honest, Ian was so young and since my exposure to male dancers was non-existent at that time, it had never occurred to me that there was anything special under those tights. But as I considered this line of thinking, I realized that boxer shorts would in all probability leave rather a conspicuous and unattractive line. Evidently it *had* occurred to Art, ever the vigilant doctor, and himself, as a former goalie, well schooled in the finer points of male protective gear. It was at that point I was introduced to the dance belt, a sort of dancer's jock strap that could not be seen under tights and left no unsightly VPLs (visible panty lines), as women like to call them. When I returned the video to Barb and told her that we had actually shown it to Ian ourselves, she was relieved. "You'll get him a dance belt, then?"

So that was her reason for showing it to us! I considered myself to have succeeded in one more ballet mom lesson and took Ian off to buy a dance belt. As I did so, I was reminded of an episode of the sitcom *Home Improvement* where Jill, the mom, takes her middle son to the sports store to buy a jock strap. Just as her son had done in the show, Ian hissed to me, "Don't ask for one; just look for it." And then, I supposed, as discretely as possible I was to pay for it. Thank heavens he was able to look after this job himself before too long.

Yes, I learned a lot of things from Frank Augustyn's television series when I finally came upon it on the Bravo! network. For that I will always be grateful to him. Some years later when he published his memoir, I would be one of the first in line to buy one and try to get inside the mind of a male dancer. Until then, I'd content myself with watching Ian dance in school recitals and generally immerse himself in character, ballet and jazz classes.

Then one day, when Ian had just turned ten years old, Barb came up to me as I waited for Ian after class.

"He really does have talent, you know." she said "One can never truly tell where it might lead, but I do think that he should audition for the National Ballet School. They'll be here for their national audition tour stop in October."

I was unusually speechless. "What exactly would that entail?" I wondered. I was soon to find out.

Act II

In which the ballet mom grows to adulthood through trials and tribulations…

EIGHT

The Real 'Billy Elliots'

"Lads don't do ballet!"
–Billy's dad, in the movie Billy Elliot

Having a son who was mad about ballet, we were mad to see the movie *Billy Elliott* when it came out in the fall of 2000. We also thought that Ian would be first in line. We could see so many parallels between our situation and Billy's. Okay, we didn't live in northern England in a small coalmining town. Art was not a coal miner nor a union supporter nor a widower and Ian was not a motherless little boy. Aside from that, we could see clear parallels.

Ian was a talented and passionate ballet dancer in a sea of little girls; indeed, he was now the only boy in any of his ballet classes. We lived in a country where "Lads don't do ballet," or so it seemed to us. A hockey-mad culture was almost as inhospitable to a boy in ballet as in a coalmining town where the boys were expected to don boxing gloves and climb into the ring. The stories clearly intersected. So, we thought Ian would want to see it. We were wrong.

After Ian saw the trailers for the movie that showed the fictitious Billy at the *barre* with a gaggle of tutu-clad twittering little girls, his blunt response was, "Girls don't wear tutus in class."

In his young mind, *Billy Elliott* could not reflect in any accurate way his experience of ballet. He and Billy had nothing in common so far as he was concerned. End of story.

When Art and I sat together in the darkened movie theatre late in September, we both shed a tear near the end. Having realized finally that his son's talent and passion were stronger than his own resolve to stop him from doing something so foreign to his family, Billy's father says goodbye to his young son as Billy leaves for London and the Royal Ballet School. I sat there, feeling quite small. When we left the theatre, I looked at Art and said, "We were the only ones in there who really knew how his dad felt."

Art nodded. We knew because I had flown to Toronto only three weeks earlier to leave my only child in the hands of strangers. We were empty nesters and our child was only eleven! That's the short story, but how we got to that day started almost exactly a year earlier when ten-year-old Ian was faced with a decision. Would he audition or not?

After Barb's surprising suggestion about Ian's auditioning for the National Ballet School, we had to scramble and do our homework. The most important question was: Did Ian want to consider auditioning for this prestigious school to which only a very small number were actually admitted–and from which a miniscule number of those auditioning stayed long enough to graduate? The latter was a fact of which we did not become fully aware until much later.

By this time I knew enough about ballet mothers to realize that most would jump at such a suggestion for their children. Indeed, there were enough such moms living vicariously from their daughters' forays into this special world that I knew any hesitation on our part to push in that direction seemed aberrant. That said, I didn't know if their reaction would be the same if they were faced with such a suggestion about their son, rather than their daughter. Trying to get Ian's answer to this question was also a bit problematic.

That autumn, several months after Barb had brought up the issue of auditioning for the National Ballet School, Ian went with his school on an overnight camping trip. Part of the school's commitment was to introduce its pupils to a number of life skills through an outdoor project that included living harmoniously with nature and learning to work as part of a team. Camping was clearly not Ian's forte. They say the apple doesn't fall far from the tree. Neither of his parents relished spending time in a leaky tent or stretching out on the hard ground with mosquitoes buzzing ominously close to our ears. After all this was coastal Nova Scotia and these issues were important. But Ian hadn't the luxury of experience to inform his decision. His hesitation stemmed from a different concern.

He got homesick; something I quickly realized would be an obstacle to a child considering living away from home for not one or two nights, but for months at a time. We could tell that he was torn by this realization. We decided to leave the issue alone for a while.

Canada's National Ballet School was a completely unknown entity to us. As I gathered information, it dawned on me that this was akin to playing in the big leagues. Famous people had gone to this school, one of whom was beloved prima ballerina Karen Kain, frequent partner of Rudolph Nureyev, who had recently retired from the National Ballet of Canada after a long and internationally acclaimed career. Frank Augustyn, now my favourite long-distance e-mail mentor, had also trained at the NBS.

The school claimed to be "a world leader in the training of ballet professionals". Who were we to argue with this? Moreover Barb, whom we trusted in these matters, had recommended this course of action. So we waited for Ian to make up his mind and I was filled with concern for him as only a mother would be. Here was my little guy struggling with such a big decision. However, as I thought more about it, although it might be opening a certain path to him, his was at that point only a decision whether or not to present himself for an audition. Getting caught up in eventualities seemed like a colossal waste of time and energy. I think that we project too far into the future. "What if he gets in?" "What if he doesn't?" "What if he hates it there?" "What if they kick him out?" What absurd considerations! He hadn't even decided to audition. That was what we faced and it was the only thing we faced.

Knowing that it was only a decision to be or not to be at the Maritime Conservatory building on a specific Saturday morning for nothing more than a ballet class conducted by teachers from the National Ballet School put things in perspective. So we waited some more. Leaving this alone was difficult for Art and me, such planners as we were.

Finally, less than a week before the audition tour was to roll into Halifax in October on its annual multi-city tour, I finally put it to him. Would he audition or wouldn't he? Since it was too late to send in an application, I would have to telephone to register him. It did occur to me that they would probably not turn away a little boy if he showed up the day of the audition, but as a reasonably sane individual, I saw no value in the drama associated with a last-minute thing. It seemed like a good lesson in making up one's mind. Finally, after some deliberation and with less than a week to the audition, he told us that he wanted to go ahead. I made the phone call to Toronto and he was registered.

That Saturday morning I drove him to the old school that housed the Maritime Conservatory. When we arrived upstairs outside the recital hall, there were hordes of little girls preening and primping with their mothers pinning numbers to the fronts and backs of their leotards. The members of the audition panel would have to identify them by number.

To fill out the registration form I sat in one of those old-style wooden school desks where the desk part grows out of the chair back and side. Returning to the registration desk, I handed it to an extremely friendly NBS staff member on the tour who took care of administrative duties.

"What time should I pick him up?" I asked her.

"Wouldn't you like to stay?" she said.

"Is that permitted?"

"Actually," she said, "we prefer the parents to stay. It's important for them to see the process."

I could not have been more delighted. Although I always wanted to be anywhere Ian was doing something, I was acutely aware of not being too over-protective. I told him that I would be staying and he seemed very pleased as he stood there looking around at all the girls. There was not another boy in sight. But as I pinned him with his No. 8, I noticed that this fact didn't seem to bother him at all. What was going on in his mind at the time, I could not even have imagined. I only knew that I wasn't going to ask him if he was nervous, remembering that conversation with the stage mom in the TV commercial audition waiting room all those years ago. Nervousness still wasn't something from which Ian suffered much, although I could tell that he was keyed up. This was a big deal to him and he was taking it seriously.

I went into the auditorium and took a seat on an aisle so that I could get a good look at the class that was to take place on the flat part of the concert hall floor down front. To the left of the open area where the children would take part in the 'class' was a long table behind which sat two women and one man, the man was holding a video camera.

The auditioning dancers had been divided into age groups; Ian would be auditioning with the youngest group. At that time the NBS auditioned children for Grades 5 through 12 for their full-time program. Since then they have dropped the full-time Grade 5. At that time Ian was in Grade 5 so would be auditioning for the following September's Grade 6 class. The truth was, however, these kids were simply auditioning for the privilege of auditioning yet again for a full four weeks' study next summer in Toronto. No decision about being invited to join the school would or could be made without that four-week audition.

One of the judges walked over from the corner and stood in front of the assembled parents and introduced herself as Mavis Staines, the artistic director of the NBS. She was a petite, slim, attractive, dark-haired woman whom I judged to be about my age. She was wearing a kind of flowing bohemian-style skirt, the kind that I love but which looks foolish on me with my tailored outlook on life. She had a beautiful composed countenance that seemed to exude patience. She didn't seem at all like the hard-hearted, cane-wielding ballet mistresses of stereotypical fame. She seemed low-key and friendly enough, although even then I felt a kind of distance. It was as if I could never really understand her world, a consideration that was undoubtedly correct.

She welcomed us and explained that it would simply be a class and that everyone should have fun. She then said to the students standing before her that today's class was only the first step in the two-step audition process. Anyone selected from today's audition would be invited to participate in the second step. That would mean that those selected would travel to Toronto the following July where they would take four weeks of classes during which time they would be evaluated on their suitability for a career in ballet. From that group an even smaller number would be offered the chance to join the full-time ballet and academic program. She was attentive not only to the audience, but most especially to the young students who were nervously twitching behind her as they waited to be in the spotlight. So it began.

Not being a dancer, I really didn't know what they were looking for. The teacher conducting the class was wonderfully friendly and caring as she went about giving directions which they all seemed to understand and then, one at a time, examining their ability to point their toes. They sat on the floor with their legs outstretched and she came along pushing each of their feet into a point. She also gently pushed their heads down onto their knees. After twenty or so years of yoga, I did recognize when someone was trying to check flexibility. What I also knew was that flexibility was not one of Ian's strong points. When he moved to the music, though, no one could touch him. He was magic. That much I did recognize about ballet.

I have to admit that I did feel a bit nervous sitting there in the audience. I've always been one of those people whose stomachs tell them when they should relax and it was doing so throughout the class. What I was truly tense about, I can't really say.

The class went on for about an hour and a half. I couldn't see the judges well because of the angle of the table where they were sitting, but I did notice the ever-present video camera focusing on one after another of the students as the class progressed. Finally it was over. Miss Staines emerged from behind the table with a demure smile and slight knowing nod of her head. She spoke directly to the students telling them that she had enjoyed very much their attention and clear love of dance.

70

"But," she said, "as much as I would love to be able to invite every one of you to come to the school next summer, we have only a very limited number of places." She gathered all of them around her in what threatened to become a group hug. "I hope that all of you will continue to love ballet and I wish all of you well." She then asked them to return to the audience to sit with their parents.

I started to put on my jacket and pick up my purse in preparation for leaving, thinking that it would be some weeks before any notification of results arrived. Then I heard her say, "I am going to call out the numbers of the students we'd like to invite to the summer audition. If you hear your number, please come down to the front to speak to us without your parents. Then we'll speak to the parents." I sat back down, clutching my purse.

By this time, Ian had arrived beside me. When he heard her say that they would be making the decision here and now, his eyes widened as he looked at me. The hairs on the back of my neck stood at attention. Oh God, I thought, immediate gratification–or not. I wasn't sure which way I wanted it to go. It was a bit like the time that we waited to see if the CBC was going to pick up that sitcom he had done at the age of four. I was thinking about Ian's ambivalence before the audition and I didn't know it at the time, but his real intention was clear later in the car when he told me that at that very moment his only thought was, "I'm going to die if they don't call my number." He was nothing if not dramatic, a quality that I'm fairly certain he inherited from his mother.

So we sat down to wait. Miss Staines looked up from the papers spread out on the desk table in front of her. She looked toward the audience. Who would be first? "Number eight, please."

Ian's eyes widened again. It was his number. He got up and walked down the aisle toward the judges who were still sitting behind the table. He looked so small but more important to me at the time, I was too far away to hear what was going on. But I did see that the cameraman was busily filming every word.

"Mrs. Parsons?"

Now it was my turn. I walked down the aisle toward the front feeling the eyes of the other mothers burning into my back.

"We'd like Ian to come to Toronto this summer," said Miss Staines when I arrived and took my place beside Ian standing over the table. "He has said that he'd like to do that. How do you and his father feel about this?"

I mumbled something about being supportive if this is what he wanted to do and thanked them. They said that a detailed letter would be coming and that Ian would still have a bit of time to make a final decision. I thanked them and we left. When I had chance, I asked Ian what they had said to him up there before they called me.

"They asked me if I got homesick."

"And what did you say?" I asked carefully, remembering the recent camping trip.

"I told them I'm getting over it!"

And just like that he was getting over being homesick. I was so relieved!

NINE

A Change of Mind

*Making the decision to have a child... is to decide forever
to have your heart go walking around outside your body.*
–Elizabeth Stone

I never really wanted to be a mother. That sounds terrible,
doesn't it? But it's not quite the way it sounds at first blush. At the
same time, I never really wanted to not be a mother. The truth is
that I always thought that if it were meant to be, it would be. When
I was in my late twenties and early thirties, I was a kind of anomaly
among my single women friends. In fact, I had one friend who was
so focused on her ticking biological clock that she married a man
ten years her junior. The only reason I could fathom for her taking
this drastic action was because of her burning desire to give birth,
and she was quite vocal about this objective. He was a nice enough
fellow, but somewhat like someone's annoying younger brother. He
was a 23-year-old engineering student; she was a 33-year-old head
nurse in a major teaching hospital and had been working for ten
years. He loved a good beer bash; she had dozens of lives in her
hands every day. I didn't quite get it. But more than that, I didn't get
this obsession with children.

I had never considered it my right to have children; rather I
saw it as a privilege. And when events did come together in my life
and provided me with my beautiful son, it was love at first sight.
In the moment of his birth, there was no doubt in my mind that I
was meant to be a mother and my feeling of privilege has never
ended. This feeling was one of the reasons that, when I returned to

73

work following a six-month sabbatical from my teaching post at the university the year Ian turned ten, I decided I wanted to have a bit more time to spend with my child before he was all grown up and left home. As a tenured professor, I had some negotiating room. I asked to have my full-time contract changed to half time, allowing me to work full-time for six months of every year, with six months to pursue my own interests, whether or not they were related to my university teaching and writing. It had never occurred to me that Ian might not even be around for me to spend more time with! What parent ever considers this possibility? Every fall we're inundated with stories of mothers (and increasingly fathers) who are coping with the loss of a child to a university dorm, but rarely do you hear of their leaving at eleven! I was now coming to the full realization of the nature of this privilege of being a mother. Now I would have to work on a major transformation of my expectations, just in case Ian did receive an invitation to the full-time program at the National Ballet School–and accepted it.

But even after the invitation to the summer school audition, there was much research to be done. In the main, we would want to visit this school and see where we were sending our child. Every year the National Ballet School presents its Spring Showcase public performance in May and offers tours of the school at the same time. We booked our airline tickets, our performance tickets and our tour time, then the three of us set off for Toronto one beautiful weekend in late May, only a few months after Ian had turned eleven.

On Friday morning precisely at eleven o'clock, we presented ourselves at the front entrance to the school for our guided tour. Located on a small cross street between two major Toronto thoroughfares, Jarvis and Yonge Streets, the school fronted the street with a series of old brownstones anchored on one end by an imposing columned building that was once a Quaker meeting house. As I stood on the sidewalk looking up at such an edifice, I was thinking how its elegant façade seemed to echo the elegance of the public face of ballet. We walked up the narrow cement stairs under a crumbling sign that proclaimed in both English and French that this innocuous little door led to the National Ballet School and entered a small hole of a reception area. This made me wonder again. Could the façade be some sort of misrepresentation of what lay beneath? It was not a calming thought for a mom who was about to pass over her first–and last–born child.

We were among a group of ten or twelve people who were taking this tour, a first glimpse behind the pillars. Truly, a larger group could not have been accommodated. It seemed to me that it was a good thing that most of those within the walls were near stick figures themselves; otherwise they never would have been able to navigate the narrow hallways and steep staircases that characterized this grouping of inter-connected buildings that had clearly had a former life as private residences.

The entire school building seemed to consist of a rabbit warren of rooms, corridors and stairways. You had to go up to go down and go down to go up, or so it seemed. Offices filled every nook and crevice including the small corridors that had been built to connect one house to another. In the central area (at least I thought it was central) there were several ballet studios that opened off a very small indoor courtyard-like place. Leotard-clad children from about Ian's age upwards milled about inside the studios and lolled on the floors and benches outside. The bulletin boards were covered with masses of schedules. Gaggles of yet more leotard-clad students, along with a few sporting the standard school uniform (plaid skirts for girls, grey trousers for boys with a white button-down, logoed shirt) were gathered around them seemingly studying the contents. And there were boys! Quite a lot of them.

They also led us to the girls' residence where we saw a typical residence room, not unlike that in any aging university residence. But they did not take us to the boys' residence. Perhaps that was wise.

The whole experience was a bit surreal.

The final part of the tour was a small-group session with the academic principal who began by announcing that she was about to retire and would not, in fact, be at the school come September. By this time we realized that there were several other parents and their daughters who were there because of the impending summer school. There was one little girl, in particular, who made her presence known.

I noticed that she had been staring at Ian quite a bit during the tour, and now as she sat beside her father while we listened to the principal, she could hardly take her eyes off him. Just as I was beginning to draw the conclusion that I had never before met such a seemingly passionate, dedicated bunch of people as were the employees of the National Ballet School, her slender arm popped up. Her father looked at her quizzically.

"Do you have a question?" asked the principal.

The little girl glanced at Ian just before she asked her question. "How many boys are in the school?"

"About a third of the students are boys," was the answer.

Then, just before the session continued, the little arm shot up again. "Do they take classes with the girls?"

"Yes, they take their school classes together and some of their ballet classes."

Before anyone could say another word there was another question. "What do boys wear for ballet?"

This was getting to be a bit much for the bewildered father. "Why all the questions about boys?" he hissed at her, waving away any answer.

I knew why she had so many questions. It was very likely because she had never seen a boy in ballet class—perhaps even in her ballet school—and when she saw Ian, she realized that this would be something new. This is the situation all over Canada. As the mother of one of those boys, I knew that their presence was a novelty—and not always such a welcome one, at least where the parents were concerned.

When the tour was over, we had much to talk about. Art and I were both impressed with the people. There was little about the actual buildings to get excited about; indeed, it was hard to imagine that they were really able to educate and to train ballet dancers to such international acclaim in such Dickensian environs. It seemed, however, that this is precisely what they did do. In the end, how Art and I felt about it would take a back seat to Ian's perceptions. Before we could come to any conclusions, though, there was one more aspect of the school that we had to see. We had to see that performance and decide for ourselves whether or not it did live up to its press, so to speak.

We arrived at the school's Betty Oliphant Theatre on Jarvis Street in downtown Toronto a half hour before the curtain. Enjoying the unusually warm evening, people were milling about on the sidewalk. At least it was unusual for us three who were more used to breezy, ocean-cooled late spring evenings. All three of us were sizing up the crowd and it was difficult for us to figure out just who all these people were. Were they parents of current students? Were there others there like us, checking things out? Were they Torontonians who had come to see a student performance? Later we were to learn that they were all of the above.

The Betty O, fondly so called by NBS insiders, is a wonderful little theatre named for one of the co-founders and first artistic director of the school. With a stage reportedly as large as that of the Hummingbird Centre in downtown Toronto–at that time the performance home of the National Ballet of Canada–it had a tiered house with a capacity of about 250. There did not seem to be a bad seat in the house if you didn't mind the fact that if you had legs more than 20 inches or so long, your knees hit the back of the seat in front. The seats were more cramped than on a charter flight and had less padding. Once the show began that didn't matter though.

As the lights dimmed a slim, dark-haired and familiar-looking woman emerged from the shadows and took up a position behind a standing microphone on the floor in front of the stage to our left. A soft spotlight washed over her. I knew immediately where I had seen her before.

"Good evening, everyone," she began softly, looking around at the audience. "My name is Mavis Staines and it is my privilege to be the artistic director of Canada's National Ballet School."

Her choice of words in her introduction struck me. The sincerity with which she suggested her firm belief that this was indeed her privilege was palpable. Her soft-spoken words and demeanour belied a steely determination that I was beginning to perceive. She said a few words about the show and then the light on her dimmed and someone came out of the shadows to remove the microphone. A pianist moved into the spotlight now focused on the grand piano on the floor in front of the stage. She took her bow, the audience clapped politely and the curtain went up.

Dance performances have always seemed peculiar to me, someone for whom words are so important. Just ask my husband and he'll be the first to say that words are, indeed, a big part of my life—both written and spoken. They always have been. However, in the dance world once a performance begins, no one speaks. For a long time I had difficulty with this since I always wanted to know who was dancing, who the choreographer was and what the music was. I couldn't see this on the program in the dark and no one was telling me anything between segments. I would just have to put up with trying to remember or perhaps let myself be swept away by the performance, so that it wouldn't matter at all. The dancers took to the stage one after the other in singles, doubles and groups of various sizes.

It was astounding. Sitting there in the dark, I could only whisper to Art, "Do you believe that these are high school students?"

To put it mildly, we were blown away. I was thinking about these dancers—all between about the ages of 15 and 18 or 19—and considered what other high school students were doing at that time. Here they were, a group of polished, clearly gifted performers who seemed to know exactly what they wanted and precisely how to get there. And they were beautiful. To a person, there was not a clumsy or homely or pimple-faced teenager among them. They were, in a word, exquisite. This is the public face of the ballet school and the ballet world at the elite level.

I watched Ian's face. He looked as if he were in a trance, his eyes never leaving the stage for a moment as the students performed. I wondered what could possibly be going through his young mind and I couldn't truly put myself in his place. I wasn't sure that I had ever experienced the kind of passion that was evident in that theatre that evening. In a way I envied it. I wondered if he could picture himself up there on that very stage and I wondered if I could picture it. Oddly enough, I could.

TEN

A Glimpse Behind the Pillars

The world of dance is a charmed place.
Some people like to inhabit it, others to behold it;
Either way, it is rewarding.

–Margot Fonteyn

Who am I to argue with Dame Margot Fonteyn? However, she probably didn't have in mind, when she divided people into only two worlds, a ballet mom about to give up her son to the gods of ballet. Does a ballet mom inhabit the ballet world? Or, does she just behold it? Our first foray into the world of the elite ballet school gave me plenty of reasons to believe that there is a kind of limbo where ballet moms come to rest between those two worlds.

It's clear that we don't inhabit that world of dance. Just ask the ballet girl or boy and she or he will be quick to say, "But you really can't understand." I sometimes wonder what children of ballet dancers themselves say. Do they tell their parents that things have changed and they cannot possibly understand either?

Then there's that other place in which the late Dame Margot suggests the rest of the world inhabits–that world where all we do is behold dance. That doesn't seem quite right to me. Indeed, I had ample reason to think that I had a larger role. And that role started a new phase on the day I left my only child with people I had never met before in a distant city in an odd, run-down residence.

It was early July and the National Ballet School's summer school was about to begin. Ian was eleven and had flown many times with us before, but never alone–yet. Of course there was absolutely no way I was going to let him get himself to that school for his very first time away from home, apart from those few school camping adventures that were memorable only for their homesickness. So, I flew with my excited son to Toronto, known to many–mostly those who live there–as the centre of the universe. I have to say, though, that despite all the Toronto-bashing that goes on in Canada I happen to like Toronto. It has always had a kind of clean-cut buzz, a bit like New York City but slightly less edgy. That said, I had never considered depositing my young son in its very centre, leaving him behind and returning to my now-empty nest. Who expects to be facing an empty nest when your child is only eleven years old? But that's exactly what I did.

We arrived at the residence fairly early and found that few other students had arrived. This was our first time in the boys' residence, and it soon became clear why they had kept visitors away from it on our tour earlier in May. It was a crumbling set of side-by-side brownstones that had clearly seen better days. Designers would say the building had good bones, I guess; lots of peeled and chipped crown mouldings, plaster walls with the odd crack and scratch, fireplaces that didn't work, sweeping staircases with disintegrating railings. But none of this seemed to matter to Ian as we made our way upstairs to the room that would be his personal space for the next four weeks. Of course he would be sharing that space with two other boys, both of whom were also auditioning for the full-time program. Today was the day for auditioning students to arrive. The returning students would arrive tomorrow; they were required to attend the July summer school every year. That's when I started to get confused.

We deposited Ian's belongings in his room. It consisted of a set of bunk beds and one other bed plus three elderly, scratched wooden dressers. As well there were a couple of extremely small desks with unmatched chairs, all of which looked like they had been rescued from the landfill. There were no curtains on the high windows, only roller blinds that didn't seem to work reliably. I was appalled. Ian was in heaven. I had heard rumours of a new residence in the works and thought it was not a moment too soon.

Then I made up his bed, replacing the orphanage-issue sheets with ones from home and topped it with his favourite blanket, so that I could feel as if he might be able to feel at home. I don't know whether or not this mattered to him at that stage, but it certainly mattered to Mom. We then went back downstairs to what was referred to as the res office. It had been the living room in the building's former life and contained an aging, sagging yet comfortable couch and chairs surrounding the non-working fireplace, a table and a desk where the house parents took audience. It felt kind of homey. A boy, probably a year or two older than Ian, was saying goodbye to his father. They hugged warmly and the father said goodbye to the houseparent in the office as if they were old friends. If this was the day for auditioning students to arrive, how did the house parents seem to know this young man and his dad so well? It was my first lesson in the realities of the elite ballet school.

After the father left, I introduced myself to the young man. He said his name was Skye.

"So, you're a returning student?" I asked casually.

"Not really," he said. "I was here for a year and had to leave because of an injury."

In my foggy lack of understanding of the processes and procedures of a ballet school, I still didn't understand. "Oh, so you're coming back."

"I hope so," he said. I must have looked puzzled so he continued, "If you leave for any reason, you have to audition all over again."

Oh. That had never occurred to me. The idea of an injury having such a world-changing impact on a young life hadn't occurred to me. It would, however, occur to me many times as my life as a ballet mom progressed. Again, I realized I had a great deal to learn.

Ian and I spent the next few hours having lunch and doing a bit of downtown shopping. We were putting off the inevitable. My flight home would leave in the early evening and I would have to get back to the airport very soon. I could feel that he was excited to be there, but I could also feel a sense of trepidation. Perhaps that was only my apprehension, so palpable between us.

It was time. I had to leave and he had to stay. I asked the house parent to call me an airport limo and we waited in the front room.

Skye had returned to the office and seemed to be at loose ends himself. One of the house parents asked him if he'd get a game so that he and Ian could hang out for a while. The house parent looked at me, and I knew that he was trying to ease Ian into the residence life, something for which this mom was very grateful. I certainly did not want to cry. I'm not a public crier in any case, but I was damn sure I didn't want Ian to feel my anxiety. It wasn't so much that I thought any harm would come to him, it was just a sense of impending emptiness. It would be some time yet before I learned the benefits of having a child away at school.

One of the school rules was that auditioning students were not allowed any contact with their parents during their first week in residence. They told us that it made the transition easier for the student. It certainly would not make the transition any easier for the parents, but then I had yet to fully realize that parents come second. We could not call Ian nor could he call us until the following Saturday. I figured it would be a long week.

The car arrived and Ian came outside to hug me. Then he went back inside to play Monopoly with Skye, and I burrowed into the squishy leather of the back seat of the Lincoln Town Car as it pulled away from the curb and turned the corner into Jarvis Street traffic. I sat as far into the corner of the leather seat as I could and wiped away the tears. As we made our way down Jarvis toward the expressway to the airport, I wondered what we had done.

By the time I reached the airport departure lounge I was over it. At least I didn't feel like crying any more. "I can do this," I said to myself. If Ian could do it, so could I. I called Art and we talked a bit about actually having a summer to ourselves. Not all was dismal.

A couple of days later, and still several days before we were permitted to talk to him, we received a fax from Ian since this was the only kind of correspondence allowed during that week and only for something really needed. Here's what it said:

"Hi Mom, Dad and Gambit [his dog]!

I'm kind of homesick. I can't get to sleep at night because my room mates keep me awake. I don't like my ballet class all that much. But I like body conditioning. Please tell me where you put the rest of my long pants...Love, Ian"

So, what's a mother to think? We were permitted a return fax to queries such as this so, as I was directed by an adult's handwriting at the bottom, I faxed my answer to the question of the missing pants. My heart went out to this little guy and for a day or two I felt a bit off balance. I didn't want to read too much between the lines–that would only get me into trouble. He didn't say he wanted to come home or that anything terrible was happening.

So I waited for Saturday's phone call. By then he was heading off on one of the many planned outings for the youngest auditioning students. Although he said he was a bit homesick, he was sleeping a bit better and things were generally looking up. He still didn't like his ballet teacher, though. His name was Roberto Campanella and Mr Campanella didn't like him, or so Ian thought. How could anyone not like my son? The man must be daft!

The next three weeks went by rather quickly or so it seemed to us, enjoying our summer on the ocean back in Nova Scotia. Then the last week arrived and we didn't know what was happening. We had been told that if our child was going to be invited to the full-time program, we would receive a phone call during the last week. Evidently, if the call did not come, we were simply to conclude that they did not want him. The first call came from Ian on Monday.

"Did you get a call yet?"

No, we hadn't received a call. According to Ian, all the students were lined up at the pay phones trying to call home to ask this same question. I asked him if he was hoping for the call and it was clear that although he was unsure of whether or not he wanted to be there on a full-time basis, he certainly did want to be asked. It seemed to be a bit of an ego thing.

Tuesday. Another phone call from Ian. "Did you get a call?"

Nothing yet. No calls for his roommates either. The anxiety was mounting. We could feel it all the way out on the east coast.

Wednesday. Another phone call from Ian: "Did you get a call?"

Finally I could say, "Yes, we received a call." The call, however, said that Miss Staines would like to meet with us on Friday when we were scheduled to arrive in Toronto to observe Ian's final class and then take him home. According to the students, any call like this meant that you were in. We decided that we would take the view that until she actually invited him, we would not be spreading the word that Ian had been accepted into the National Ballet School. But that was good enough for him. We had a meeting set. He could relax and enjoy the rest of his time there.

As directed, on Friday we dutifully arrived at Miss Staines' office without Ian. She was warm and friendly and made us feel welcome. We took our seats in her small office and waited for her to speak.

"We'd like to have Ian join us here for the full-time program," she said and I think Art and I both breathed out simultaneously. Had we actually been holding our breath? Perhaps we had, at least figuratively. Why we were so keyed up about this can only be explained by our connection to our child. Whether or not he was to be accepted didn't really make bit of difference to us, or so we naively thought. We still thought that he was going to attend university and be a lawyer or a veterinarian or something. Why else did we have that registered educational savings plan?

The rest of the conversation focused on the process and timeframe for making a decision. Ian had about two weeks to accept or decline the offer. Truthfully, we didn't know what decision he would make. I think, in the interests of complete honesty, there was a little something in me that wanted him to have this experience, –to say, "Yes"– despite my not knowing yet how I would cope. I knew only that if this was what my child needed to do, I would certainly do nothing to stand in his way. Prepare the child for the path, not the path for the child.

Next was a meeting with the administrative director of the school, Robert Sirman, a well respected arts administrator who guided the school's excellent fiscal record. He sat us down and basically told us that a contract with the school, which we would be required to sign, would bind us to paying tuition, residence fees, uniform expenses and anything else that the school dreamed up as required. We assured him that we could handle this and would not be applying for financial assistance. Then we settled back for a chat about the school's ambitious fundraising drive to renovate old facilities and build a new school. The plans were grandiose, indeed, and they were on their way to raising the necessary dollars. For a moment I wondered if ever we would see or be a part of the new facilities.

Then came time to discuss the decision with Ian. We had the rest of the weekend in Toronto and when we told Ian about the firm offer he was very excited. This excitement, however, seemed to do little to move him toward a decision. "I'll have to think about it," was all he would say about any decision.

We didn't want to push. But we were in Toronto and being the practical, plan-ahead kind of people that Art and I were at that point in our lives, if Ian did decide to take them up on their offer, we knew that he would need to be fitted for school uniforms. It would be much more difficult to accomplish that after returning to Halifax. We had the packet of information for new students so we suggested to Ian that we go out to the store that provided uniforms for the students to get measured in case we had to order them after we returned to Halifax. We knew that it was a bit sneaky on our part. We knew that it would push the decision to the front of his mind. So, sue us. Unused to not being in control of the decisions, we didn't like being kept in suspense, especially by an eleven-year-old. We still wanted it to be his decision, with our input in areas where he needed help.

He did tell us that help would be welcome. Oh, where's that fine line between encouraging and pushing? It's a difficult one, indeed, to walk. It's truly like being on a tightrope. One false step and you're over the side—one side or the other; you can never be sure at the outset.

We rented a car and took the parkway to a suburban strip mall and the uniform supplier. With the help of staff clearly used to this sort of thing, we found the appropriate grey flannels (that weren't really flannel, rather washable polyester that would withstand the school laundry), white shirts and green sweater. He took everything into a dressing room and we waited. And waited. We had assiduously avoided the topic of any decision, wanting to let events unfold as they were supposed to.

We waited outside the dressing room for him to appear and to give us some idea of size so that we could take those with us for possible future reference. Just as we were beginning to wonder what was taking him so long, the dressing room door opened dramatically and Ian stepped out the door in full National Ballet School regalia.

"I've decided!" he said, quite spectacularly, standing up tall. "I'm going!"

We were quite surprised by this. It seemed he had stood in the dressing room studying himself in the mirror before emerging. We had not expected a decision so soon, or such a vehement one.

"What made up your mind?" we asked innocently.

"I just thought that if I didn't take this chance, I would never really know if this is what I want to do."

It was quite a revelation for an eleven-year-old and quite a correct one. We bought the necessary uniforms, returned to Halifax and sent back the letter confirming his acceptance.

I had been worried only that if he turned it down, he might always wonder, since it was clear that he *wanted* to dance. The question that they would help him answer was whether he *needed* to dance.

ELEVEN

Long-distance Mother

*A mother is not a persona to lean on
but a person to make leaning unnecessary.*
–Dorothy C. Fisher

In September I once again left my son on the sidewalk in Toronto, feeling only slightly less queasy than I had two months earlier. I never really doubted, at least not consciously, that Ian would be all right. By October, however, I thought I had an ulcer. By November I found myself starting a journal, both for archival and cathartic purposes. Truth be told, it was more cathartic than anything else. I think that I had read too many magazine articles about parenting because I harboured some kind of deep-seated belief that I should be more involved in my son's world. I should be helping him with his schoolwork. We should be sitting down as a family for dinner most nights; we should be sharing our stories of our days. I should be kissing him good night. I can almost hear that needle screeching across that broken record to indicate clearly that I had to get off that thought process. But it was tough.

He did call with a piece of exciting news about three weeks after school started. We had been told in a memo that had arrived in the mail in early September or late August, not to make any arrangements for students to come home for Christmas until casting for *Nutcracker* had been done. A large number of young National Ballet School students were used every year in the National Ballet of Canada's production. It was a tradition.

We didn't quite understand what that would mean for us if Ian was to be a part of this production until he called to tell us that he was on the cast list and that the final show wasn't until January 3. January 3! That would mean that he couldn't come home for Christmas at all. It was an easy decision; we'd simply have to go to Toronto and that was all there was to it. What would it be like? So many new things affected our whole family unit. Ian didn't have any problem with changing long-standing family Christmas traditions, and we were secretly giddy at the thought of missing another Christmas Eve with extended family for every such gathering seemed to be a clone of the one the year before. Moreover Ian was more focused on having this opportunity to be on stage with the company dancers at the Hummingbird Centre in downtown Toronto because the students did more than stand on stage holding things–they actually got to dance. He was elated, so how could we do other than share his elation? It was a good thing he had this to look forward to since there were so many other little frustrations and hurdles in that first full term away from home.

November 10, 2000

...I miss him a lot...since he left I've experienced such a range of emotions. I feel proud, sometimes even elated that he has such a passion and a talent. I feel sad that I'm not a daily presence in his life. I'm occasionally angry if I think his ballet teachers are being unnecessarily harsh–which seems to a far-away mother to be their way. I feel excited along with him for his accomplishments. But he is experiencing what most university freshmen face–a crippling workload, mild homesickness, occasional questions about what he's doing there, frequent exhilaration at a singular accomplishment– but he's only eleven!

There were times that fall when I wondered if we had done the right thing, encouraging this foray into a world that, in truth, we knew little about. Indeed, how could anyone really know about that world if they hadn't been part of it? These musings were really only a superficial manifestation of long-distance mother guilt. In my heart I knew that we were doing what we must.

The school encouraged the children to get out of residence and home for Thanksgiving in October if at all possible. This would be the first time that Ian would fly by himself. We felt that we had done our best to prepare him: he had flown with us many times already in his eleven years. Even though the airline had an unaccompanied minor escort service, I felt a bit stressed about it. Art thought I was crazy, but he tolerated with good humour my motherly concerns (and he'd have to continue in this way for a good many years!). We arrived at the airport in plenty of time to meet the arriving flight. As we had directed him, Ian had dutifully telephoned us from the departure lounge at Pearson International Airport in Toronto where he had been deposited by a staff member from Air Canada, a service covered by the additional $40 that we had to pay for his flying alone. When we checked the flight, we could be assured that he had probably made it aboard. I knew he'd be safe with an airline escort all the way to the bottom of the escalator where we waited anxiously in a throng of families and business associates–all awaiting their own people.

As I stood there I thought about how a year earlier I could not have foreseen that I would be separated from my young child for such a long time. I was also thinking about the twice-daily telephone calls that I'd been receiving from Ian. These did make me feel a bit more connected with him than I otherwise might have, but the calls were a double-edged sword.

Although I thought I wanted to know every detail of what was going on, I was not there and could not be there and, therefore, could not have the same control I thought I would have had were he at home. This was especially difficult whenever he told me that his roommates were bugging him, or he couldn't sleep, or he was having trouble getting his homework done, or that he was constantly being criticized in ballet class. This last one was truly challenging for a kid who had been the star at his previous school, as had all of the children accepted into this elite school.

Although I was happy that he kept in touch so closely–or as closely as he could–I occasionally wondered if this was a sign that he was really, horribly homesick. He never once, however, suggested even in an oblique kind of way, that he regretted his decision or that he wanted to come home. That's because no matter what the school threw at him, he knew he wanted to dance. On the positive side, every once in a while he was asked to demonstrate something for the others. This never happened in class, however, only in rehearsals for *Nutcracker*.

Naturally, as I stood waiting to see him come down that airport escalator, I was filled with a sense of anticipation. Would he tell us things that would be hard for us to hear? Did he love it? Hate it? Not care? Perhaps that would be the hardest one to deal with. Finally, we spotted him.

There was eleven-year-old Ian making his way down the escalator with the crowd of disembarking passengers, all towering over him. His face lit up when he saw us and he made his way toward us through he crowd. He was not too old to hug us in public! But, wait a minute.

I looked around. "Where's your airline escort?"

"Oh," he said shrugging, "I just got up with everyone and got off the plane. I knew where to go."

I didn't know whether to laugh or to be angry at the airline for seemingly abandoning a child who was on his own for the first time. All I could really do was laugh and be happy that he had flown with us before. So, based on his experience, he had had the self-confidence to realize that he knew exactly what to do.

It was a terrific visit, but two days later we had to take him back to the airport and say goodbye again. It would become a familiar activity.

The first weekend in December, we set off to Toronto ourselves for the annual Parents' Day. It would consist of meetings with all teachers, both academic and artistic, a student performance and a parents' meeting, something they had started only recently. Our eyes were opened to a number of things that weekend in Toronto.

It all began on the evening before our teacher meetings when we picked Ian up at the boys' residence to take him out to dinner. We made our way up the narrow staircase to the second floor where he shared a room with two other little boys, one of whom I personally found particularly annoying. Not unlike the room he had occupied during summer school, it was small but I had never seen a boys' residence room after occupation. It looked like a battlefield–and they had lost both the battle and the war or so it seemed.

It was a room probably designed to accommodate one or at the most two people, but had three beds, three dressers, three little tables that I think were supposed to be desks but were so buried under debris they were barely visible. Moreover, it had no closet space to speak of. The vintage of the building was such that it was built long before the idea of fitted closets was popular. This created a real problem when three eleven-year-old boys, responsible for their own belongings, tried to live in a tiny space together.

There were piles of clothes and books on every imaginable surface. Was anything clean? There were little balls of clearly dirty, stiff socks here, a terribly dirty white–or what was once white–ballet slipper there. There were black ballet trunks here, a white school button-down shirt there. "I'll wear that one tomorrow," said Ian. We shook it out and rolled our eyes. And don't even get me started on the dust balls. According to Ian the school cleaning staff vacuumed the room weekly. I couldn't figure out how they managed to vacuum anything since there were no empty surfaces!

We managed to make a first pass at cleaning, but I found it difficult to see how anyone, never mind a child of mine, could live like this. Art, a neat freak if ever there was one, had a particularly difficult time with this. In fact, after that weekend, only once or twice at most did he ever climb the stairs in the boys' residence, preferring instead to avoid the inevitable stress that he experienced when faced with such mayhem.

The good news was that we were not the only parents who found this difficult. When we returned to Ian's room with him later, we found one of his room mates with his father and his sister, methodically but gingerly picking up little socks and other articles and saying, "Clean or dirty?"

When a mother considers her beautiful home and the lovely, private room and bathroom that her son has at home and compares this to the facilities that could only be described as wretched, it almost makes her want to weep. The only thing keeping her from that kind of a response is that the son seems actually to like it!

I had been looking forward to meeting his teachers since it was already December with the first term drawing to a close, and I hadn't met even one of them. At home, I would have met the teachers in September. This was perhaps one of the most difficult aspects of long-distance mothering at this early stage. I felt very much on the outside of my own son's life, much as I tried to be helpful to him over the phone. When he called about homework problems, I was frustrated since I was so far away. It would take me all year to get over the feeling that I should be a bigger part in my son's academic life. In fact the meetings with the teachers, especially his main Grade 6 teacher, suggested that he wasn't working up to capacity since he didn't always complete his homework on time. After seeing the state of the residence, it was a wonder to me that he got any homework at all done and that his marks were as high as they were. They were really more than adequate–just perhaps not so high as if he had been at home with parents prodding every day. (Come to think of it, perhaps that's not the way to parent anyway!)

The meeting with Ian's ballet teacher was, if possible, even more trying. Ian was blessed with what we perceived to be a gem of a teacher–older, very experienced, motherly–Carole Chadwick, the head of the junior school. And yet we found the meeting to be wholly unsatisfying. We sat in her tiny office, knees almost touching, and she told us that Ian needed to be more consistent. He needed to be more flexible. He needed to feel his body more. What were we supposed to make of this? We had no idea, but pressed on.

Finally, after much subtle prodding on our part for some sense of outcomes, she grudgingly admitted that he was making some progress. I supposed that this was a good thing–but then again, I couldn't be certain. It was exasperating to two parents who always felt in control of their lives. It was clear that in this situation we had no control. Even more maddening was the fact that, although she was telling us this, we could not in any way help our young son. All we could do was encourage him to do his best and continue to love dancing. So that's what we did. After the meetings with the teachers, the school had arranged for all the parents to meet in the theatre. From what I could glean, this was a very new approach to communication with the parents. There had only been one or two such previous meetings. I was curious about what had prompted this addition to the lines of communication. I could only imagine that in the 1990s parents began to become more annoying to a school where they could begin to feel that they didn't count for much more than to pay the bills–a truth that was revealing itself to us day by day.

We stood in the lobby before the meeting began chatting with the only other parent that we actually knew at that point. Elizabeth was the physician whom I had met in Halifax at the boys' ballet classes a few years earlier; this was now her son's third year at the school and he still loved it. She was the mom who had experienced the same problems at the dance school in Halifax that had validated my early observation that boys were not all together welcome in the regional schools, or that at the very least there were very few teachers who seemed to know what to do with them.

Elizabeth was giving us a heads-up on the tone and depth of the previous meeting. "It will likely deteriorate into a parents' discussion of the availability or non-availability of carrot sticks for snacks if it's anything like the last one," she grumbled. "And the kids don't even want them."

It seemed to me to be less than substantive if we were to be treated to such a mundane discussion, but it also occurred to me that this was no doubt a kind of reaction to the lack of day-to-day control that parents had over children's lives–something that most parents take for granted. So we took our seats and the meeting began.

This year was to be different, said Mavis Staines from the stage. The school's consulting psychiatrist, Dr. Richard Meen, would lead the gathering. He would make a presentation and then we could discuss issues raised if we so desired.

Dr. Meen stood and walked to the microphone. He arranged his pages and placed a hand on the podium, leaning into his audience. I liked him at once. He was a substantial man, so even if the previous meetings had not been substantial, this one was sure to be different.

At that point in our relationship with Ian's school, we were unclear as to the role that Dr. Meen played. Did these kids need psychiatrists? Were they somehow troubled? They seemed a fair questions since Dick Meen's day job was running a facility for youth-at-risk troubled teens to be sure. It seemed that the school had recognized a few years earlier that these gifted children were under unique stresses. Thus, in an effort to help them avoid the kind of personal problems that can arise from this level of stress and from their own artistic gifts, the school instituted meetings with counsellors of various sorts, with Richard Meen as its outside expert and coordinator. It was obvious that Canada's National Ballet School was at the forefront in its approach to the realities of modern ballet students and their training.

Dr. Meen's presentation that day was titled "Becoming a Ballet Dancer: A Family Affair." He began by relating a story about a meeting he had recently had with a group of Grade 10 and 11 boys, a regular occurrence for all students. As Dr. Meen told it, at one point during the meeting one of the boys remarked that he just wanted to be treated as if he were normal. One of his classmates immediately quipped, "Forget it. You're not. We're not." So began Dr. Meen's reflections on our abnormal children.

What struck me initially was his candour at the notion that now, after a number of years with the school, he realized that it was somewhat disingenuous to try to create normalcy in a situation that was clearly a far cry from a normal adolescence. It seemed to me that this had not been his initial assessment of how to handle the situation. Indeed, he said, "I interpreted passion to be obsession." He had now realized that the talent and potential greatness of these students, as he saw it, made for a situation that had to be dealt with as unique. However, it was his next remark that made us sit up and take notice.

"I now know that the normal, average young person who comes to the National Ballet School is not likely to make it as a professional dancer and will never achieve the status of being a great ballet dancer."

In other words, the ones who make it will without doubt be labelled as different, exceptional and gifted. Of course, these different, exceptional and gifted children were going to make their parents anxious. I was right there with him on that one. How could a parent ever be certain that she was doing the right thing?

When he said, "There is nothing worse for parents than feeling, or even being, impotent when their child is in pain and they know that there is nothing that they can do." I felt the tears begin to build. I swallowed hard and wondered how he had managed to get inside my head.

For some time after the meeting I thought a lot about Dr. Meen's words. Art and I discussed the meaning of having a child who does not take the well-worn path and we concluded that it was a privilege and less of a problem for us. We felt that we had been presented with a gift that had to be nurtured. Now, if only we could figure out how to do that.

If I ever worry about what will happen in the future, I think of Elizabeth, who continued to be wracked by the notion that this is abnormal. "What are we letting happen to our children?" she said later.

I thought about her words, too, and wondered if we really had any right to not let them dance anyway.

TWELVE

So the Ride Begins

Life is a long lesson in humility.
–James M. Barrie

On that fateful day when I had left Ian at the National Ballet School in September, we had stepped onto the roller coaster, and it took off even before we had a chance to catch our breath and get a firm seat. We were doomed to spend some time trying to get seated and to find a comfortable position. Comfort was something I personally never really did find. Rather, I came to a kind of understanding of what my role was (and was not) as a mom, and the role Art and I as parents might play. Eventually we were consoled by the realization that we were part of something bigger than all three of us, but that would not happen in that first year. So we hung on for dear life, ignoring the odd bout of queasiness.

Coming home after that first Parents' Day gave me much to ponder. As I reflected on the experience, I realized that my roller coaster just might be on a bit of a smooth section.

December 20, 2000

It's pouring rain this morning, coming down in buckets– whatever the expression. Rain in Nova Scotia in December is dreary, but somehow makes me feel right. It wouldn't be right to have a snow storm. I'm starting to feel a bit more settled. I've been rather unsettled to say the least, having lost my child to the NBS. After our visit two weeks ago, I said to Art that I had a strong feeling that he's not mine anymore

(was he ever?), rather that he belongs to the world. I suppose
every mother has to get to that realization, but I suspect the
acknowledgement is usually more gradual. For moms with
kids like Ian, it comes right up and slaps you in the face. It's
a feeling of pride and loss at the same time. It's a feeling that
you've not quite finished something.

That was five days before Christmas–a Christmas that would be
very different for us in so many ways.

After Ian's call about casting in *Nutcracker*, we had to break it to
our families on the east coast that we would be spending Christmas
in a downtown hotel in Toronto. People consoled us, but we were
actually excited. Only three weeks after our Parents' Day adventure
we packed our bags again and headed back to Toronto.

Just one year earlier, after we had attended the local production
of the *Nutcracker*, memorable mostly for the fact that there was only
one male in the cast (no surprise there), we had told Ian we would
take him to Toronto to see the National Ballet of Canada's production
the next year. It never occurred to us at the time that not only would
he be in Toronto for *Nutcracker*, but that he would be in it.

Nutcracker is one of those ballets that even non-ballet fans seem
to find captivating. For some people it is a holiday tradition, a kind
of ritual that is not to be missed. Indeed, every region seems to have
its version and even in those places where there is no real ballet
company, they seem to find a way to put on some semblance of
the beloved story with its music so synonymous with Christmas for
many. In fact, Ian had been the sole boy in the version put on by a
small ballet school outside Halifax the year before: they had come
looking for him since he was one of the few boys in the province
who actually danced. So he had been their ten-year-old *Nutcracker*
prince. But this year was to be very different.

Replete with spectacular costumes and sets, the National
Ballet of Canada's version is often reported to be the best in the
world. I for one cannot argue with that. It was relaunched in 1995
with choreography by the internationally renowned choreographer

James Kudelka, the National Ballet's Artistic Director at the time, and the famous music of Tchaikovsky. When we finally did settle into our seats in the second row of the Hummingbird Centre, the word 'spectacular' didn't even come close to describing this wonderful production. I was delighted that principal dancer Rex Harrington performed as the *Nutcracker* prince that evening. This compensated for my only disappointment in my current exposure to ballet: I would never get to see Canada's treasured and internationally acclaimed Karen Kain perform since she had already retired, as had her partner Frank Augustyn, whose work had helped me in so many ways as I learned to be a ballet mom. But sitting close enough to the stage to be hit by drops of sweat as Rex Harrington himself thrilled the audience was good enough for me. Other than that, and the overall impression that it was beyond breathtaking, I seem to have seen little of it.

The next morning at breakfast with Ian at the hotel, we discussed the performance. Art and Ian kept asking me if I had seen this or that in the family scene during the first act. "What?" I kept asking. I saw only Ian when he was on stage. There might as well have been no one else there.

At first it was hard to pick him out. The costumes were all so fantastic and colourful and Ian wore a red wig, Cossack pants (this version is firmly set in its original Russia) and tattered jacket for his role as part of the poor family. Once I had honed in on him, however, he was unmistakable among the other children. It was such an odd feeling, seeing him up there on that massive stage with professional dancers. As I watched him, it occurred to me that he might be up there one day dancing the part of Peter, the prince, or maybe Uncle Nickolai, the other major male role. But it was clear from my discussion with Art and Ian that I would have to find a way to focus less on my own little dancer and more on the whole cast if I was to really experience this production.

We did have a wonderful hotel Christmas with as much family as I would truly enjoy–just the three of us. As I sat in the hotel's hot tub on Christmas day I marvelled at how preposterous it was that at this exact moment, were it not for my talented child, I would be at home in my kitchen, leaning over a hot stove basting a turkey.

Before the trip was over, I had another chance to see a bit more of the ballet. It was not finished its run until after New Year's, so Art had returned to his office full of patients, and I had stayed behind for the final few performance days to go home with Ian. He would have a week off before he had to return to the school. I had tickets for the final performance. I sat in the restaurant at the hotel that afternoon before the show watching the snow fall gently outside the glassed-in dining room, trying not to wonder if our plane would get out after tonight's performance. I was ready to return home. But the sun came out late in the afternoon and I went by myself to the ballet once more. This time I noticed the little girls in the audience, all dressed up in lace and velvet toting their Barbie ballerina dolls and wondered what it was about ballet that fascinated them. It surely wasn't the same thing that kept a young boy dancing in the face of so many pink tights and tutus. It started me wondering if the allure of the ballet for little girls had more to do with the costumes and the tutus–a princess fantasy.

Finally, it was over. I was able to go backstage (they still allowed parents this indulgence in those days) to wait for Ian after the final curtain and the company's bows. No one knows how to take a bow better than ballet dancers for they learn this very early. In fact, they bow at the end of every class, although it is referred to as *reverence,* in thanks to the teacher and pianist, I suppose. I happened to arrive backstage just before the end of the next-to-last scene and watched as the ballerinas rushed into the wings after their performances.

"F**k! That was awful!" said one of those ethereal creatures. Now I knew where Ian had acquired his colourful speech.

When Ian eventually emerged and we met the car that I had arranged to take us to the airport, it had started snowing again. It was beautiful; that is, if you weren't anxious to get on a plane and get home. By the time the plane left it was really coming down, but it did take off and we were home just after midnight. Ian hadn't been home in months but within days he was suffering from dance withdrawal, listening to the *Nutcracker* CD and dancing at every opportunity. Sadly, his one week of holiday time was soon over and we put him on another plane headed back to Toronto. I missed him all over again.

THIRTEEN

A Wild Ride

*...I don't remember a great deal of positive
reinforcement from my days at the school. Of course,
that, too, is the ballet tradition...*
–Karen Kain, *Movement Never Lies*

Over the next few months I found myself reading Karen Kain's memoir and highlighting a couple of her observations about the school, one of which is above. From time to time when Ian called with his woes about this teacher or that student, I tended to see all of this through the filter of a mother's almost powerless concern. (And to be fair, it must be said that Ms. Kain does go on in her book to suggest that there may have indeed been positive feedback, but her perfectionist approach to her art made her hear only criticism. A mother is a bit like this when it comes to hearing about her child, I fear.)

I often wondered about those kids, all eleven years old, and how they really felt about the experience. Before Ian went back to school in the new year, we warned him about the possibility that one or more of his classmates might not return. When he called us that first week, he told us that we had been right. One of his classmates had decided that this school was not the right place for her. In fact, he said that six had left since the year started. This was news to us. It was also news to us that the kids had been talking about these departures and that several others seemed to be harbouring similar thoughts. When we visited Ian in February to celebrate his twelfth birthday, it became clear how these kinds of thoughts could be uppermost in students' minds.

Ian had taken us upstairs in the old brownstone that passed for a boys' residence to the small room that he shared with two other boys. He was now in a different room than the one in which we had visited him before Christmas. The school's policy was to do a room change at the end of every term. Initially sceptical of this upheaval in the lives of the students, I soon began to realize that the residence staff members were wiser than me. Indeed, they had so many more years of experience dealing with these adolescents. As it turned out, there were two very good reasons for this: the first was that not all the rooms were identical. That meant that some of the boys had only one room mate and others had as many as four—hardly an equitable situation, although as they got older and therefore bigger, the more space logically went to the seniors. Just one pair of size eleven men's shoes could practically fill one of their all-too-infrequently available closets! The second reason was probably even more sensible: if a student happened to have a room mate (or two or three) with whom he or she did not get along particularly well, this situation could be counted on to last for only one term. When kids live together in such close quarters for such a long period of time, there are bound to be issues. So, this was a new room.

A set of bunkbeds was crammed against one wall, with little room to get into the very tiny closet space. Just like in the previous room, each of the three boys had a very small desk that served as a catch-all for school books, clothes, both clean and dirty (little had changed since December), pens, papers and just about anything else that didn't have a home. One of Ian's new roommates was very messy, the other very tidy. Ian said he was somewhere in between. However, what really struck me the most was the white board that hung over the desk of one of his room mates. On it in very large letters were the words, "I miss my mommy." This child was two years older than Ian and he was clearly feeling the loss of his family. Like some kind of surreal wallpaper, letters from his family plastered the walls surrounding his white board. Later when I casually commented to Ian about this, he said, "He's already decided he's not coming back next year. He misses being a regular person." Pow! It struck me again, and I was reminded of Dr. Meen's presentation and wondered how deeply this lack of regularity affected the kids.

Ian was a bit bummed out by all this talk of leaving. It would, however, become a recurring theme in his life at the NBS. He would lose friends every year that he was there–some of their own choice, many others because they would be asked to leave. We would just have to be there to help him to deal with whatever we could–from a distance.

As a 21st century mom, I thought it seemed only reasonable to expect that my child's school would be a safe, nurturing place–and I'm a typical mom in that way–and it seems especially important when the school is required not only to fulfil those educational needs, but has to be a home away from home as well. However, when your child is at an elite ballet school, this is the case only part of the time—or at least that's how it came across. I sometimes wondered if the environment was at least a part of what some of the students couldn't cope with. I suppose it might be a reasonable expectation that they acclimatize to it since their ballet world in the future would require such adaptation. As I was remembering this part of that first year, I had wanted to call this chapter "Bullies in the Ballet School," but that seemed somehow mean-spirited. Although, to tell the truth, there were bullies–and not where you might expect to find them.

I might have thought that Carole Chadwick, Ian's ballet teacher, was a bit of a bully if I had let myself interpret her actions in this way. Ian called last night to ask me to help him write a letter to Miss Chadwick. He thinks he needs one-on-one tutorials. (I'm not sure that they even do this here.) He thinks that she has already written him off, that she has already decided his fate for this year. I'm having a hard time figuring out exactly what Ian wants to do since I know he has mixed feelings about staying versus leaving. All I can do is go with the flow and try to help him figure it out–without getting too involved. When I asked him how he got this idea, he said that he overheard her say to one of the student teachers in his class, "Don't bother correcting him". Ian thinks that she

*believes that he is not interested in applying corrections. He
says that they never actually tell him if he is doing anything
right at all, but they just berate him if he does it wrong. The
rest of the time he says there is nothing.*

This revelation came on the heels of another incident that
involved acting-up. Ian and one of the other boys in his class
were evidently horsing around before class early in the week. As
Ian explained it to me, it seemed to me that they were just being
pre-adolescent boys. (But here's the mother-at-a-distance talking
again.) Miss Chadwick was annoyed and sent them to the academic
principal's office. I wondered what the principal would be inclined
to do with them. A seasoned academic with a graduate degree in
mathematics, at first glance this newcomer to the school seemed an
unlikely candidate to be the principal at a ballet school. However,
we needed to keep in mind that he had come from a school where
he had dealt with students who were gifted academically, and he
was in charge of ensuring that these students eventually graduated
from high school with diplomas that would allow them to go on to
university if they so chose. This was an important part of the NBS
educational philosophy. He also had a daughter who was a student
at the school but several years ahead of Ian.

According to Ian's report to us later, the principal did little
with them other than require them to sit in his office for a while,
presumably to contemplate their behaviour. All this did in reality,
however, was cause them to miss the entire ballet class, something
that both of them could ill-afford. Art and I soon realized that this
was the precise moment at which Ian began to perfect his use of
the pre-emptive strike. When an incident like this occurred, before
anyone in authority could get to us, he would call and give us his
version. The call from a principal or residence house-parent would
never come as a surprise. Thus, we were always inoculated against
any alternative perceptions of the incident that might be harboured
by those authority figures–an inspired approach for any adolescent,
in my view.

So, I took action, something that I was finding difficult and that would take me some time to overcome. I put in a call for Miss Chadwick to discuss all manner of perceived hiccups from the preceding week. I wanted to hear from her own lips that she had already given up on him.

When she did call me later I drew a completely different picture...

It seems we don't have a problem at all. Thirty minutes on the phone with Miss Chadwick (who always seems dependably reasonable) and I, too, am convinced that Ian is experiencing what she terms "a wrinkle." He and Adam were booted out of the ballet class on Monday for misbehaving, just as Ian had said, and they then missed the whole thing resulting in them floundering for the rest of the week. This is what prompted her remark to the student teacher. She says, however, that he had a beautiful, focused week and she knows he can do it. "Even his socks and shoes are cleaner," she says–clearly an important issue!

So if the teachers weren't really bullies, then where did I see them? All I had to do was look around his class and what did I see? A group of catty, competitive prima donnas? Well, this is how I saw them at the time. The girls in his class could have won a prize.

The bullying had started early in the year. I had been listening patiently to Ian for months about how the girls were treating him. Specifically, I was hearing about how the Grade 6 girls, his classmates, behaved. By all accounts he was getting along swimmingly with the Grade 7 and older girls. I knew that Ian liked to have fun in school. He was a gregarious, out-going boy who often had trouble keeping quiet. He always had a lot to say in his academic classes in the past, and we realized it was because he liked to participate. Ian was no wall flower when it came to discussions and activities. I must say that we encouraged this kind of fulsome involvement in school activities. Ian liked to joke and sing and hum–and he did like to tease. Evidently, this didn't sit well with the budding ballerinas; they didn't find him funny at all. The result was a class visit from the principal.

As Ian related it to me, the principal came to the classroom and spent some time talking about respect, and Ian said, "Everyone knew he was talking about me." When questioned over the phone about his perceived lack of respect, as he described his behaviour to me, I knew immediately that it had nothing whatever to do with respect of his fellow students or lack thereof. It had everything to do with how he was trying to relate in a situation where he had few guidelines.

Later, the girls complained to the teacher that Ian was repeating himself. Again the teacher sent him to see the principal who told him to try to just keep quiet for two more days since spring break was at hand. Then the principal told Ian that he was harassing the girls. Indeed, when I spoke to him on the phone later, he used that word in describing to me Ian's behaviour. That's when I called time out.

"Stop right there," I said to him. "You want to be very careful of your use of a word like harassment."

I was becoming angrier by the minute. To all appearances we had a boy here of whose individuality we were very proud. His behaviour was being misinterpreted by a group of girls. *Their* bullying was more of the passive-aggressive nature than of the direct aggressive kind. They chose to whine to a teacher who then sided with them regardless of Ian's explanations. At least that's how he related it to us, so far away.

There was no doubt that, from where I sat, Ian didn't fit into their prim ballerina mould. Rightly or wrongly, as a mom that was the only reasonable conclusion I could draw. The fact that Ian's teacher and the principal himself sided with the girls without exploring the situation further made me first worried, then angry. I did wonder briefly if the principal might not be a bit biased since he himself was the father of a budding ballerina–not among those in question.

It was hard from a distance not to conclude that Ian was having to deal with a gaggle of prima donnas. In conversation with the principal, perhaps my characterization of his classmates in this way was ill-advised, but no more so than his harassment remark. That's the kind of label you don't want put on your boy at the age of twelve.

Was I being overly sensitive? Maybe, but not being there to sit down in person with both Ian and the teacher made it very difficult not to take Ian's side. From time to time, all of this made me wonder whether this was really, truly the right path for him.

Ian had thought about that path, too, as only a twelve-year-old boy might. As we neared the end of the year, it became clearer that Ian wanted to be asked to return to the school the following year–even if he himself didn't know if he would take them up on it.

About a month before we were to hear the verdict for the year, Art and I made another trip to Toronto for the annual music night. This visit gave the school another opportunity to host a parents' meeting, again chaired by Dr. Meen. Being a modern mom who still often tried to keep up with the latest on parenting, I looked forward to his take on a topic that was high in my mind at the time: adolescence. But he had a sort of spin that had not occurred to me.

With his tongue planted firmly in his cheek, he suggested that adolescence usually begins around the age of fourteen and ends at death. Ha, ha, I thought. Yes, we all have the adolescent more or less still there in us. Some of us try to bury it, while others embrace it and, like Peter Pan, seem never to grow up. But he was deadly serious when he suggested that our current culture tends to prolong this period so that, in his estimation, adolescence was not expected to end until age twenty-five or even thirty these days. I sighed in recognition of what I had seen in my own classrooms at the university. The level of maturity among freshmen was considerably lower than it had been in the early years of my career as a professor. But where did that leave us parents of these abnormal children?

Then he dropped the one bomb that stayed with me for many years to come. "The ballet world, however," he said from the stage, "I believe requires an eclipsing of the process to somewhere around sixteen to seventeen years–often before most parents are really prepared to wave goodbye and wish their child well on his or her journey, alone."

There it was. I was on the edge of my seat. In this world of ballet, my child would be expected to be out of his adolescence by age sixteen or seventeen. I would have to wave goodbye to him. He would have to make his way. Alone. I had not really been prepared to begin thinking that way. I then added that thought onto Dr. Meean's suggestion that my child was making his way through the mysterious world of adolescence within yet another shadowy world, the world of ballet where my child would not be doing it the same way as my neighbour's children might. In Dr. Meen's words that day, "They [the neighbour's children] are not ballet students. They are not by choice living in an androgynous world and aggressively moulding their bodies into artistic instruments." He suggested that some have compared it to the long-banned Chinese practice of foot binding, referring to this life as cruel and abusive.

Elizabeth's words echoed in my mind. "What, indeed, are we letting happen to our children?"

I thought a lot about that crash course in growing up that Dr. Meen cautioned us to be aware of and to embrace. My child would grow up so quickly, perhaps more quickly than I would evolve as a mother. I was just getting the hang of having a preadolescent around, and now he was telling me that I'd soon be the parent of an adult if Ian kept on this course. The discussion that followed his presentation was clearly focused on the notion that we'd have to give up the idea that these kids were going to pursue higher education if they were to be ballet dancers. I hadn't thought of that. Studying at university was, for us, a natural progression from high school. But, if a dance career is a real possibility, we were told firmly then and there that upon high school graduation these kids would be looking for jobs. And some of those jobs would be many miles away, even on other continents. Such was the international possibility after graduation from an elite ballet school. All this would take some getting used to.

FOURTEEN

The First Verdict

For behind all seen things lies something vaster,
Everything is but a path, a portal, a window
Opening on to more than itself.
 –Antoine de Saint-Exupéry

I have always believed that whenever one door closes, another door opens. So why did my stress level begin to rise as we moved toward the end of that first year of having our child away at school? Why was I drawn to–or perhaps sucked into–the quicksand of a decision over which I had no control? I guess it's because I had expected to have much more control over my young child's life than this. How obtuse can we be? Truly, who does have such control over their child? It would have made little difference had we been told that he had cancer or some other chronic disease. That would have put us squarely on the merry-go-round of the health care system. Instead, we were on a different kind of amusement park ride: the roller coaster. And there were certainly highs and lows.

There had been the low of the confrontation with Miss Chadwick and the harassment issue. There had been the high of seeing the entire school perform in the annual music night–not to mention his duet with a classmate, Ian's pure soprano voice carrying the day. There had been the incident of the floor mat fight in the ballet studio– another chance for Ian to practise the pre-emptive strike. There had been *Nutcracker*. There had been the academic report that he was not working up to his potential. Yet there had also been our genuine delight in a report card telling of B's when he could do A's, but for a kid on his own with no parents to help with homework or to nag him to even get it done, we were quite happy.

Then late in the afternoon, one day early in May, the telephone rang.

"Mom, guess where I am. I'm in the other building." The voice was a whisper. The other building to which he referred was the theatre building, the Betty O, a place the younger students like Ian were not allowed to be on their own. "I came over alone and my body conditioning teacher just came in. If he finds me, he'll ground me. I have to run and hide in the boys' washroom until the other guys get here."

"You're supposed to wait for the others, aren't you?" I said, trying my best to be stern rather than either panicked or amused, both of which emotions surged. What was he up to and why didn't anyone know where he was? And...why was he calling me to tell me about his misbehaviour?

"Yes, but it's so silly. I come over by myself all the time."

"Does anyone know that? You know the rules are there to protect you." As if that would make a difference to a twelve-year-old clearly testing his boundaries.

"Yeah. Courtney (one of the girls' house parents) caught me once and told me not to do it again. I'll really get grounded this time." He paused for just a second or two. "Here come the Grade 5's! Got to go. Bye Mom!" *Kiss, Kiss*. Click.

Grr...! What was that all about? Clearly it was another pre-emptive strike and I should be very annoyed at him for flouting the rules. We'd have to talk, but to tell the truth beneath it all I was a bit relieved to recognize that deep within that little artist-in-the-making there was a mischievous young boy testing his independence. He kept just enough of a lifeline to us so far away so that we could reel him in if he started to get in over his head. Perhaps that was the reason for the call. His need to act out just a little was balanced by his need to feel that he had a safety net–another revelation to me.

When I told Barb, Ian's old ballet teacher and now a fellow

member of the Board at the Maritime Conservatory where I still continued my volunteer work, she said that stars are usually the rebels. I was relieved, stupidly, for the feeling was short-lived.

A week later we were heading solidly down the home stretch of that first year.

"It's cruel and unusual punishment," Art said one evening after dinner as we sat having a glass of wine in the living room overlooking the cove. We had been discussing the latest nasty rumour circulating within the Grade 6 ballet-student world: that NBS parents were to be treated to a particularly torturous approach in informing them of the decision about their children.

Indeed, it was a bit more than a rumour. We had received a carefully worded memo from the school's artistic director telling us that we would be informed of their decision regarding reacceptance of our child during the week before the long weekend in May. According to their perspective, that would allow those students who were not being invited for another year to spend the weekend home with their parents, and to return the following week to spend the next four weeks seeking closure. Wow, I thought, that's got to be hard. Clearly, though, this was necessary to finish out the year. The timing was thought to allow enough time to make other arrangements for the following year. Yikes! If Ian was not going to be reaccepted or should choose not to return at this stage, I had no idea where he would go to school. He had been attending the Shambhala School the year before, but it wouldn't be a simple matter of showing up again. That window of time was just enough to cause me considerable anxiety. I had yet to learn the virtue of not worrying about things that might never happen.

The particularly nasty part of the rumour about how the parents and students would be informed was this: if our child was going to be reaccepted, we would hear nothing at all and should just assume the best; if the school had decided that they did not want Ian to continue, at some point that week we would allegedly receive a phone call during which we would be asked if we wanted to inform him ourselves or have them do it. It seemed unbelievable to me that we would have to wait on tenterhooks all week and make assumptions otherwise. So, the week began.

On Monday evening at 7:30, an hour or more before our usual nightly call, the phone rang. "Did you get a call yet?" were the first words out of Ian's mouth. No, we had not received a call. It was hard to tell if he was relieved or not, but he had a more in-depth story to tell.

According to Ian, earlier in the day he and his classmates had been subjected to an hour-long discussion of the reacceptance process and how they felt about it. One of the students asked Miss Chadwick if the staff already knew decisions about each of the students–a reasonable question from a young student–with an equally predictable response. Of course as decision week began, they had to know already. Miss Chadwick replied that yes, they already knew.

"It feels really weird now," Ian said to me. He felt odd to be in her class at this juncture, subjected to her corrections, all the while knowing that she knew and he did not.

I tried to put myself in his position and considered how I would feel if I knew that someone knew something about me that I didn't know. I felt powerless, a most uncomfortable and increasingly common feeling for a woman who had prided herself on being in control her whole life. The issue of the power imbalance was even more acute at this time than any other time that year. It was not only the imbalance between the child and the teacher–an expected one– but also the imbalance of power between the school and the parent. Ian then asked me to call him immediately if I received a call. The students had been told that if their parents didn't get a call by the end of the week they could assume that they had been reaccepted.

"I told Miss Chadwick that my mother doesn't like to make assumptions," he said.

He was echoing words that he had heard me utter on more than one occasion so far in his short life. To this Miss Chadwick evidently had no response.

Monday

Ian's rationale for wanting me to immediately put in a call to him is that he can be mentally prepared, knowing what to expect when he next calls home. Then, each time he himself calls home, he knows he won't face uncertainty. It's that uncertainty that seems to be eating away at him.

He and his room-mates are not taking a fatalistic approach, though.

"Twelve of the grade eights say they're not coming back anyway," he says.

We'll see, I think.

Oh–this is hard! I'm trying to take a laissez-faire attitude toward it myself. What else is there to do? I'm displeased and perplexed about this approach, but...oh-oh, the phone is ringing. Not the NBS this time! I really don't expect to get a call...they haven't given any kind of real substantive warning... but still... A mother's issues are a mother's issues regardless of the circumstances of her children. I'd like to be there to help him through this stress. On the other hand, maybe it's not really that stressful for him.

Naturally, Ian called again on Tuesday evening and I just let him talk. The students all seemed to be sure that Miss Chadwick had let up on corrections in class for those who were not being asked back. It seemed as if the students were playing a macabre game as they tried to figure out who was or was not a target of her perceived waning interest. I'm sure, though, that this was the only way it could reasonably be done in the students' minds.

After his rant about this situation, he whispered, "Don't say a word, Mom, but Curtis got a call today." This of course was code for he has been booted out. Curtis was the roommate who seemed to be missing his family even more than most.

Wednesday

I return from my yoga class this morning to a message on the answering machine. The voice is Carole Chadwick's.

117

"Please call me back," is all she says.

I look at the phone for a moment before picking up the receiver. Then I punch in her number. She isn't in. And so I leave a message and I wait. I will probably have to wait hours, I think, since I know that she teaches Ian's ballet class right after lunch.

So, this is it? The dreaded call. Or will the call be about some other permutation or combination? All I can do is wait. I call Art so that he can share my misery!

4 pm: The call finally comes. I'm a bit sad, I think. But they say they don't think he's quite "ready." He's not focused enough. He's not physical enough. They think he could benefit from a year or two at home with his father and me. We'd like him to go home and miss us, they say. He doesn't need to be here just yet. He could audition again for the following year.

The 'they' on the other end of the phone were Carole Chadwick and Mavis Staines on speaker-phone. They seemed to think that perhaps Ian possibly still had some potential, but he would not be returning to NBS next year. I must have sounded to them like an idiot on the line. I could barely put two coherent words together since my mind was racing in a million directions at once, a clear example of monkey mind if ever I had experienced one.

My first thought was, My God! Where will he go to school? Is it too late to get him back into Shambhala? Surely after three years in private school and a year at a ballet school the public school system was not the place for this child. Will he go back to the Conservatory? Will he even want to? I had heard that such a decision from an elite ballet school often chases the dream right out of the child. Will he be devastated when I tell him? How can we help him through this disappointment? Is it even a disappointment? When they mentioned the words '…audition again', I thought, Auditions are in October–so soon. How will he know whether or not to audition?

When I called Ian, his first question was, "Why don't they want me?"

So I talk a bit about what I understand and then wait for his response. It is immediate and matter-of-fact, as if I should perhaps have known all along.

"Call Barb. Tell her I'm coming back." Obviously there was no decision that the National Ballet School could make that would strip this child's passion for dance.

Although I was trying not to, I must have sounded a bit off. "You sound disappointed, Mom," he said, picking up on something across the miles.

I couldn't tell him that I was disappointed at the changes that were surely going to come in our lives. In spite of missing him, we had truly enjoyed our regular trips to Toronto. With this level of commitment to his ballet and other performing arts, we would have to have just as high a commitment. As well, the boarding school approach had not been without its clear benefits. Ian did seem a bit overly enthusiastic about coming home; then I remembered his ambivalence.

Ambivalence. It was the one thing, according to Carole and Mavis, for which there was little room. This, despite Dr. Meen's message only a month earlier that a bit of ambivalence was to be expected, and was perhaps even healthy in these talented kids.

To be fair, one of the most important things that Mavis Staines said that day was, "We often see this in boys. If he keeps stretching, he doesn't need to start this early. He could come back in a year or two."

I thought this might have been easier to accept if they had said that he didn't have the talent to become a ballet dancer.

I wasn't the only one who was disappointed. Art was as well. But, we had to make sure Ian didn't think it had to do with his performance or talent. It was more that we were disappointed in the inevitable changes that we were facing. We both felt a bit melancholic, but the veil of melancholy didn't last long. Ian came home for the weekend and having him actually in our presence gave us the feeling that things were unfolding as they should. We adapted.

While he was home, it became clear to us as parents that Ian had been dancing for Ms. Staines, Miss Chadwick and who knows who else–but not for himself. His delight in dancing was being diminished. The NBS almost succeeded, perhaps inadvertently, in wringing all the joy out of his passion for dance. He had stopped dancing for himself. Perhaps if we could help him get back to that, he could follow his passion to new heights.

So, with our admonition in his ears that he spend the next four weeks dancing for no one but himself, he got back on that plane with a smile on his face and, two weeks later, called to say he'd had such a fantastic class that day. Miss Chadwick had even said, "You're doing really well, Ian. Why didn't you do that before?" Hmm… I wondered, What would she think if she knew the reason?

FIFTEEN

Invisible

*There is nothing like returning to a place that remains unchanged
to find the ways in which you yourself have altered.*
–Nelson Mandela

The last weeks of Ian's residency at the NBS were upon us. He telephoned daily, voicing mixed emotions that seemed to reflect our own feelings. His relationship with Carole Chadwick seemed to have improved over the past months, a development whose irony was not lost on us as we wondered, What next?

Thursday, June 14, 2001

We leave for Toronto later today to attend the closing ceremonies–such as they are—at the National Ballet School. I'm feeling oddly like I seem to remember feeling on February 11, 1987, early in the morning just as we were deciding that it was probably time to leave for the maternity hospital and have this baby. I knew then that when I returned to my house, life as we had known it would never be the same again. I feel like we're bringing home a new child. Sure, he's been home for visits through the year and we've been there to visit him, it's never been more than a week and he's not the same kid I left on the Toronto sidewalk ten months ago. I was talking with my sister who as a mom of three knows a thing or two about mothering. When she said, "You'll have to get to know him again," I was irritated. I'm thinking–I still know my child, we keep a close relationship across the miles. But now as I begin this journey to bring him home, I think that perhaps she might be a little bit right.

The end-of-year activities at the school were to be our chance to say farewell to everyone. We were headed to Toronto to view Ian's final class and a year-end performance of character and folk dancing. The youngest students were not permitted to perform any ballet in public. I guessed it was because there were standards to be met and young students didn't meet them. I was reduced to guessing since the school, it seemed, saw no need to share with parents their reasoning on any artistic issue. This only highlighted for me my on-going disappointment with the school's lack of performance opportunities for the youngest students. An important part of the joy of dance for Ian and for many of his classmates was the opportunity to be in front of an audience. It seemed that the school had a different view. They had a reputation to uphold and their students needed to be of a certain calibre before they were ready for public consumption, or so it seemed to us, but we were really only guessing. Since no one ever talked about these kinds of things, we had to draw our own conclusions. This unanswered question was added to another bit of information that Ian shared with us one evening before the end of the year.

"They're creating technical robots!" This was Art's vehement response to the news from Ian that Miss Chadwick had recommended to Ian's ballet teacher in Halifax that he return home and take classes toward the Grade3 Royal Academy of Dance level, ostensibly "... for the technical training." However, Ian had completed this level before he had gone to Toronto! Ye, gods, I thought. He passed that exam over a year ago–with commendation, no less! What the hell had we just spent $22,000 for a year at the NBS for? They told us that he's making progress. *This* is progress? We were wild, but had no one to whom to complain.

As I tried to look at this objectively–difficult perhaps, but not impossible–I considered that maybe they really did think he had talent and that this recommendation really would strengthen his underlying technique. How were we to know? This prompted Art to suggest we try to book a few minutes with the artistic director while we were in Toronto this time; and this is when we really started to feel invisible.

It moved imperceptibly; nothing specific really. Actually, it had begun right after 'the phone call.' It was an odd feeling, probably a commingling of both what was really going on in the NBS world and our feelings about it. There seemed to be an ever-widening space between us and the school and between Ian and the school. The form letter exacerbated it: "This letter serves to confirm…the school's decision to not reaccept Ian for professional ballet training beyond the current year…" Couldn't they have hired a PR writer to spin it a little? But that was not the school's style. A decision had been taken and they had moved on. We ought to get on with it and move on, too. Formal to the end.

Art and I talked and realized that we were in no position to know what to do for this child. Should we be looking for another residential school? Should we continue to encourage this talent? Should we get a second opinion? Should we try to get an audition with the Royal Winnipeg Ballet School to see if they'd take him this year? Or, should we just go with the flow and enjoy having our boy at home? We decided that a meeting with Mavis Staines might help us to better understand our role. So, I called her and left a message on her voice mail.

My answering machine received the reply. However, it was not from Mavis herself at all. "Ms. Staines asked me to call…" said the disembodied voice of Miss Chadwick. Ms. Staines would be too busy to see us while we were in Toronto. Graduation day would be upon her and all the rest of the activities involved in meetings with those students whom she *did* want to have at the school the following year. We'd have to get in line and take our place at the rear. Perhaps they could set up a conference call next week?

Art's reaction was the same as mine: Why bother?

We'd figure it out for ourselves. Suddenly a feeling that all would be well came over me, and I knew that we just had to pay attention to our child and follow our hearts as he followed his. Art and I knew that we would have needed to be eyeball-to-eyeball with Mavis. We needed to sit across from her–in person. That's the way we liked to do those kinds of things. So I called Carole Chadwick the next day and declined her kind offer.

...We often don't know the exact moment when a feeling starts to creep up on us. And whether we're willing to pay attention to that feeling and ultimately believe its truth, that doesn't change its meaning and ramifications. Our children do not belong to us. This child does not belong to me. And I'm reminded of that poem from my young adulthood–"The Desiderata." It says, "You are a child of the universe..." That means me and more importantly right now–that means my son. It's up to me to pay attention and hear that truth.

The ending was a bit of a blur. We watched his class. He seemed as good as any of them. We watched his junior choreography–and we were blown away. Using a group of five classmates, including himself, Ian had created a work to the music of Mary Jane Lamond, a Nova Scotian singer whose work had been unfamiliar to everyone it seems. Her Gaelic music was foreign to them. As a leader Ian worked with his group to come up with the only real, non-derivative piece of choreography presented. The assistant teacher came to us after the class presentation in the studio and told us that Ian's piece was the most developed and mature. At least he might have a future in creating dance.

After the class, Art left the studio for a few minutes and I had Carole Chadwick to myself. That's when she told me that Ian was, in her words, "...very talented." If he could just find his focus, they'd welcome him back. There it was. Finally. Now we had something to go on.

We sat that afternoon watching what the school called at that time the junior-school closing. Before the presentation began, Mavis Staines took to the microphone and as was her habit, introduced the program. The main theme of her remarks puzzled me until I was able to ask Ian about it after the show. She seemed to be saying goodbye. According to Ian, over half the junior school had not been invited back the following year. I was, as they say in England, gobsmacked.

This was one thing no one ever tells you. In fact, it took many years before even our friends understood that for a child to stay in the school, he or she had to be reaccepted every year. Getting in was only the first step–quite a small one at that.

Finally, it was over. The students gathered in the room outside the stage door and the tears flowed freely. Ian, however, was dry-eyed. He took one look around at the meltdown, swung his backpack over his shoulder and said, "Let's get out of here."

As we walked past those tall pillars of the building that had come to symbolize the National Ballet School for us, Art said, "I don't think we've seen the last of this place."

I looked up at the pillars and knew that he was right.

But life went on, and in some ways we were not invisible to the NBS. The day we returned home from Toronto with our child in tow, we received a letter on the NBS letterhead. It began, "Dear Dr. & Mrs. Parsons, As NBS parents..." and went on to ask us to give them some more money. We were not feeling overly generous at the time, needless to say. Our apparent parsimoniousness would pass.

So we began a new routine with a child who had grown far more sophisticated than his peers in that year away from home. As I mentioned, part of my education as a ballet mom had been to answer the call of the board of governors of the Maritime Conservatory. In that capacity I found myself as the liaison between them and an upstart private school called Kings View Academy. Indeed, it was my suggestion that Kings View rent space from the Conservatory since the latter needed the cash since it had a tenant leaving–another school- that had rented several classrooms and shared auditorium space. My motives were not, however, all that altruistic. I saw this marriage as a terrific one for Ian's needs: a private school that treated each child as an individual that was located in the same building in which he would be taking hours and hours a week of dance classes. Add to this KVA's desire to carve out a niche as the place for arts-infused curricula coupled with its desire to create an integrated music and dance program, and I had reached Nirvana. I acted as matchmaker and the marriage duly took place. Ian had a place to go in the fall.

That made the next year very easy to revert to our family life that had begun to veer over that year of an empty nest. Art and I started to get used to it, and I stopped worrying what Ian would do with his life. After all, he was twelve years old. But my complacency as a ballet mom would not last long.

By mid-August Ian was well into dance intensives at home and studying now with guest teacher Owen Montegue, a former principal dancer with the National Ballet of Canada. It seemed Owen had a knack for pushing Ian and getting him to work harder than ever. His inspiration seemed to be something that the NBS had lacked. In fairness, though, a lot of growing had gone on, and there is a time and place for everything. It became obvious that Ian again started thinking about the NBS. Occasionally I found him with his yearbook, and I knew that he missed his friends. One day he casually asked me if he returned to the NBS and graduated but then decided that he didn't want to be a classical ballet dancer, "Would you and Dad think that you had wasted your money?"

It was an interesting question. To me, as a mom, he was thinking of his future but had not yet concluded that he wanted that straight and narrow path. Now my job would be to keep quiet and let him figure it out. I remembered that last day in the NBS residence as we ploughed our way through the debris that was his residence room. There was, amid the dust balls and dirty socks, a pair of pristine ballet sneakers, lovingly cared for and stored in their muslin bag– testimony to the kind of reverence he had for aspects of his art.

A late-summer parent-child heart-to-heart uncovered for us that Ian had never wavered from his desire to be a performer. That much was certain. He had a passion that could not be quashed. What he was dealing with now was a vestige of ambivalence about a career in classical ballet. At the last parents' meeting in May when Dr. Meen had taken to the podium, he told us that ambivalence was a healthy thing. This was in direct contrast to our interpretation of the message from the artistic staff at the NBS who, in our view, had definitely indicated that Ian needed to rid himself of that ambivalence and to focus on a path. The questions remaining–which path and to which goal–remained. It seemed so odd to be having these kinds of discussion with such a young child, and yet we knew that if he were to take that path toward a ballet career, there was little time to waste. We were not pushing for it in any way. I still thought he'd make a great lawyer and evidently so did his English teacher at KVA that year.

We watched our son with great pride that summer and early autumn as his ambivalence dissolved into clarity. Ballet, he began to discover for himself, was his real goal. Now, all he needed to do was make a decision about the path. Over the next month, he told us, he was going to decide. I held back from having any influence at this stage. It was hard, but in the end it would be the only way and I knew it. Finding myself far too caught up in the minutiae of my child's life, what I needed to do was get some perspective. It came from far away.

September 12, 2001

Yesterday, four jetliners were hijacked in the US. Two suicide-collided with the World Trade Centre in New York. The towers are no more. One hit the ground in Pennsylvania. One bombed itself into the Pentagon. All I could think about was all those poor people. And how glad I am that Ian is not at the School of American Ballet in New York. How happy I am that he's home right now.

Talk about perspective! Life is short, how short we never know. This said I needed to go with the flow.

September 19, 2001

I happen to hear Ian on the phone today with a friend he'd met at the dance intensive last month.

"No," I hear him say, "I'm going to the audition instead." He is adamant when he tells me about the conversation later. "I have to go back," he says dramatically. His friend has been wondering if he plans to go to the National Ballet School workshop that they would be hosting during the national audition tour when it rolls into Halifax next month.

"I have to go back, Mom," he is saying. "I swear I

127

saw Judy's name written in the street. And I saw Josephine walking down the street and I saw Miss Chadwick driving in Halifax. And I've seen Miss Holmes [his academic teacher at the NBS] I don't know how many times! I've even seen one or two house parents."

He's so dramatic–clearly he sees a message for him in all this.

The audition was upon us before we even knew it. This time it had a very different feel. Ian knew what he was getting into–and this time so did his mom. The stakes were higher now but according to Barb, "He's impressive," and that's just what he planned to do: impress the NBS auditioners.

In spite of Barb's assessment of the impact of his individual presentation, Ian came home the week before the audition saying that she had told him not to get his hopes up. Art and I were furious. One thing we had always tried to do for Ian was to inculcate in him a desire to prepare for success rather than for failure and then to deal with whatever happens. After our display of dismay, Ian assured us that he was still planning to do his very best and that if they didn't take him, it wouldn't be because he didn't try. It was so hard to know what was going on inside a child's head.

A beautiful autumn day dawned for the auditions. The sun shone and there was a hint of crispness to the air–sweater-weather we call it here on the shores of the Atlantic. Art made waffles, wished Ian luck and I drove him to town. On the way we picked up his friend Freddy, who was like his big sister. A classmate of his at KVA, she was living away from her family so that she could study ballet with Barb. She planned to audition with the older group that day. At seventeen and with only two years of ballet training, as terrific a dancer as she was on the local level, she knew the odds were stacked firmly against her getting into the NBS. After all, she was about to enter Grade 12. As she had received some positive feedback at workshops, she decided to present herself. This would be Freddy's first audition for anything.

We pulled up in front of the Halifax Ballet Theatre Association where the audition class for the younger students was already underway. We walked in behind Ian's friend Lee and her mother. Lee, too, had attended the NBS summer school the year before but had not been invited into the fulltime program. She, like many others, would try again.

Brenda, my first contact with the NBS two years earlier, greeted us. It was good to see a familiar friendly face. Ian and the girls got their numbers that had to be pinned to their fronts and backs and went off to warm up. Now, all I had to do was wait.

The audition began. It was so different this time. There seemed to be so much more riding on it. This time I knew enough to spend at least half my time watching the auditioners' faces.

Students lined up in three rows to begin, Ian at the far end of four in the last row, and I saw one of the auditioners smile and nod at him in recognition. I didn't know either of them, but they knew Ian, calling him by name, rather than by number. I thought how nice that was for him. Then they began.

It began with the candidates standing, staring ahead, as the judges examined body structure and proportion; each row in turn– first the front, then the side, then the back. Then one of the teachers gave instructions and the class began. The judges looked, wrote furiously, videotaped. Class started with exercises in the middle of the floor. Since there were four rows of about four each, it was rather a large class–Ian again the only boy. When they finished the centre exercises, they sat on the floor and the teacher went to each in turn, pushing down on the pointed feet. It was fascinating to me since I felt I understood slightly more this time round. Then the teacher pushed each into extended stretches, once a struggle for Ian. I was amazed at his progress in a few short months. Upon leaving the NBS in June, he could barely even touch his toes. Summer sessions had done him a world of good. Then it was his line's turn to move to the front.

I had never seen him dance better. He looked confident, princely

129

even. I decided then and there that if they didn't take him back I would never in my life know what they were looking for. I watched the kids and the judges.

Of the eleven girls with Ian, most were decent enough dancers, but to even the barely-initiated the differences became obvious. Half way through I noticed that the judges barely glanced up from reams of paper spread out on the long table in front of them while at least half the dancers were still performing. They didn't even look. They didn't need to for they had already decided against them. By the end of the 90 minutes I had picked out four myself and thought, "These are your four." But I wasn't making the decisions.

After five minutes of chatting among themselves while the kids talked quietly in the opposite corner of the studio, the head judge gathered all of them in a huddle. "As you know,"she began, "our school is small. We'd love to be able to take all of you." She was letting them down gently. "But we can offer summer school places to only a few of you. I do hope all of you enjoyed the class." They nodded. "I'll tell you the numbers of those I'd like to stay behind and the rest can go. And thank you for showing your interest."

Then softly she said the numbers. Did I hear Number 12? I wasn't sure, but judging by the look on Ian's face, I did indeed hear his number. He came over beaming as we waited for his turn to be interviewed. I was thinking that Art had been right. We had not seen the last of that place. Ian was on his way back.

After the official invitation, Ian and I headed back to the car and made our way to the nearest Tim Horton's to buy lunch to take back to Freddy who had yet to have her turn with the older auditionees. On the way, there in the car alone with me, Ian said, "Well, that was the 90 minutes that just decided the next six years of my life. I'm going back next summer and now that I know what they want, I'm going to work my butt off and graduate from the NBS." He had finally made up his mind about his future. He knew.

I did go back and sat through the second audition to see Freddy. She was very nervous and could hardly eat the sandwich we had brought. Only four girls in this audition, they were all sixteen and seventeen and trying to do the impossible: they came from small regional programs in little Nova Scotia and were trying to join the Grade 11 or 12 class at the NBS. Freddy did so well, but I could see from the judges' faces that almost from the very beginning of the audition, they seemed to have made up their minds that they would not offer even one of them a further opportunity. The audition was short and the requirements complicated. One of the girls almost burst into tears at the *barre*, she was so frustrated. She stood for a moment with her back to the judges, her hands on the *barre* and facing the mirror. I almost cried for her myself. For four young women, this would be a dream that would not come true today.

Later in the car on the way home Freddy, who at least had made it to the end of the audition–and admirably so–expressed her concern about her future. The audition had made her look squarely at what she really did want to do with her life and led her to face the fact that she would need to make some decisions.

I was so proud of my son–both for his performance and his support of his friend. He didn't wave his success that day in front of her face, but told her she had given it her best. I know that he was proud of himself. I was proud, too. And this was the first time that the NBS had been so complimentary. There were murmurs all around of how phenomenal he looked. It was an auspicious ending–and beginning.

Act III

In which the ballet mom matures to an understanding
of the role she was destined to play
—and the one she was not...

SIXTEEN

Home

We worry about what a child will be tomorrow,
and yet we forget that he is someone today.
–Stacia Tauscher

Ask any mother where she thinks her child's home is and she'll look at you as if perhaps you are suffering a temporary loss of your senses. I knew exactly where Ian's home was when he was ten years old. By the time he was thirteen, the distinction between here and there was becoming a bit blurry. With those kinds of thoughts in my mind, I set about revelling in having 'my boy' home at least for a while. While other moms grimaced at the thought of teenagers, I threw myself into it since I didn't know how long he would be with us. We settled in nicely to a great year ahead without worrying too much about what might or might not be.

I was teaching, working on a new book and trying to be there as much as possible for Ian. Art spent so much extra time in his office in the late afternoons and evenings, waiting for Ian's classes to end so that they could drive home together, that I'm sure his patients thought he slept in his examining room.

There were new things about ballet that I even began to understand a bit. One of the most striking was that there is a ballet culture, a sort of sub-group in society that you don't even know exists until you're a part of it, even if only in a peripheral way. When you're a part of it, it seems to be everywhere. When you are no longer a part of it, it might just as well not exist; it has left your reality. Having Ian home brought me closer to learning about a few of those ballet culture idiosyncrasies.

Up to this point, the issue of the ballet uniform was not a conscious concern. Ian had complained from time to time about the black shorts that the youngest boys at the National Ballet School were required to wear. My understanding was that bare legs allowed the teachers to watch the muscles closely as they developed or did not as the case may be. For the same reason, the girls had to wear pink tights. But it had never been a big issue. It became increasingly clear that the issue of what ballet dancers wore in both studio and during rehearsals was an important cultural phenomenon. Indeed, every ballet movie I had ever watched caused me to wonder if they ever thought about it at all. They all seemed to be wearing tatty, torn things that were well past their best-before dates. Even in photographs of Rudolph Nureyev in rehearsal at the height of his career, and presumably wealth, he wore tatty tights and his ever-present knitted cap to keep in the heat.

"I have to put together a rehearsal outfit," Ian said one day while maniacally rummaging through closet and drawers.

It was slim pickings, though. It's hard enough to pick up the required boys' clothes for dance around here. Evidently ballet students are not required to wear their studio uniform at rehearsals, and it seemed that the older and more shrunken the outfits got, the happier they were with them. I found this an interesting revelation about dancers: when the audience sees them on stage, they are in costume and so perfectly put together. Even when playing ragamuffin characters, such as Cinderella might be imagined, the hair and makeup are just so. Perhaps the scruffy rehearsal is a way to rebel. Or, perhaps it's for luck. I never really did find the answer.

Having Ian home that year let us parents see another side of our son–a side other than that of Ian the ballet dancer. It was exciting to see that he still pursued other interests, one of which was his singing.

Early in the fall of that year, at a board meeting of the Maritime Conservatory of Performing Arts, one of the voice teachers who was also a member of the budding opera association in the city, asked me if Ian might be interested in auditioning for the role of Amahl in the

Christmas production of *Amahl and the Night Visitors*. Unfamiliar with this opera, I was gratified to learn that it was some forty or more years old and written specifically for early television by Gian Carlo Menotti. In addition, to our great happiness, we noted it was exactly an hour long, originally made to fit into the TV scheduling framework, and all in English.

Ian was more than interested, heading off to the audition with great enthusiasm. All that fall I watched him grow ever more anxious that he be cast as Amahl, never a foregone conclusion even if you had been invited to audition. The call finally came and he did get it. At thirteen, with the ever-present knowledge that he might any day no longer be a soprano, Ian sang his heart out.

What an extraordinary Christmas gift! As parents, Art and I could have asked for nothing better from our child. We had been looking forward to seeing his performance and when it finally came just as the Christmas season approached, it was nothing short of breathtaking. Amahl is the story of a young fatherless 'cripple' whose poor mother is visited by three wise men on their way following a bright star. They seek refuge for their weariness in her modest home and Amahl is eventually cured just before he, too, goes off to visit the newborn King.

There were several performances in Halifax and we went to every one of them. On Saturday before Christmas we drove Ian to Wolfville in the Annapolis Valley where the snow was piled high. Less than two hours' drive from here and there was snow! How wonderfully holiday-like since we had none. We dropped him off at the theatre bordering the beautiful Acadia University campus and set off for lunch at one of the local wineries before the performance.

Later, in the theatre, settled into my seat, I found myself doing what everyone says you do at operas: I cried. When he sang "Don't Cry, Mother Dear" I felt as though he were singing directly to me. I glanced down at a group of women several rows below us in the bowl-like theatre, and I could see tissues in every hand. All of them were crying. Perhaps he was singing for all mothers.

At that moment I knew that this was the reason he was home that year—to give us this gift.

Art and I were not and still are not big opera fans. In fact, when a female soprano begins on a high note in an aria, the hairs on the back of my neck begin to twitch and I have the urge to cover my ears; not really polite among *operatti*. At that stage of our lives, the thought of our son's becoming an opera singer had as much appeal as if he had decided to pursue hockey. As a matter of fact, I thought I would have preferred the cold mornings in community hockey arenas. In the end we were spared.

Ian told us that every night before the performance he prayed this would not be the day his voice changed. Once he had hit that first high note, he always felt better. But very soon, as he turned thirteen, the day did come.

Ian continued to take voice lessons at the Conservatory and we didn't really know that his voice had changed until one afternoon in the spring. His wonderful teacher, Cheryl McCarthy, had been diligently preparing her students for their spring recital. We took our places and looked over the small program. This was for Cheryl's students only on this particular day. As always, we were looking forward to hearing Ian and the rest of her terrific singers.

Ian had not said a word to us about what he would sing, preferring as usual to have his performance a wonderful surprise to us. I wondered later if I had noted a bit of a sly smile as he went to the front and took his place beside his accompanist at the grand piano. When he started to sing my jaw dropped. I looked at Art's wide eyes. I think this might have been the most surprised I had seen him since the day he realized that Ian was a dancer. He, too, was slack-jawed.

Ian's voice filled the room. He was no longer that little boy soprano whose pure tones had filled the theatre in Wolfville and the church in Halifax where he had also sung Amahl. He was a baritone, a good one! He could still sing. Even today as I have watched my son grow into a young man and have seen his vocal performances get stronger and stronger every year, I still think of Cheryl and thank her for what she did. So many young boys stop singing when their voices change. She guided him through so that he could continue to enjoy music in that way. It didn't matter that he wasn't going to be a singer when he grew up, but at the end of the year Cheryl presented him with a special award, an award to recognize he had progressed from being a DWS to an SWS. He was no longer a Dancer Who Sings. He was a Singer Who Sings and, for a vocal teacher, it meant all the difference in the world. It meant a lot to my son, too. Perhaps it was one of his proudest moments. It certainly meant a lot to a mom.

Having Ian at home also put me face to face with a dilemma that I had not quite resolved.

Before the first term at school was over, Ian had begun to wonder why he had to learn math when he clearly intended to pursue a career as a dancer or, at the very least, as a performing artist of some kind. Short of saying, "Just buckle down and do it," we tried to explain the importance of learning to think in various ways; how this ability could serve him well in his life. It wasn't that he had been struggling with it, he just didn't like it. We knew that over the years many studies suggested that musical training helps with math, and I think that this was the case in Ian's situation. Apart from his reluctance to memorize the times tables, figuring out the mathematical questions didn't pose much of a problem. He just didn't see the value of it.

"Well, the academics just aren't that important, Mom!" he said. Yikes! He was such a bright kid. He learned easily, read well beyond his grade level and his wonderful grade seven English teacher, Mr. Deveaux, whom I credit with teaching him to write essays and take exams, thought he had a bright future as a lawyer because his logical thought processes were in tune with that way of thinking. And he could think on his feet, a useful skill in a litigator, in particular.

Not many months later when, one evening after we had pushed him to complete his homework, he said, "I may never go to university, you know," it was like a sword through the heart of a university professor mom who never thought she'd hear those words from her offspring.

Intellectually, I understood that his path might not take him in that direction, but since I had been programmed to believe that formal education didn't end with high school, it was difficult. Then Dr. Meen's prescient words about dancers' eclipsed adolescence and their moving so quickly into the work world rang in my head. Art, the physician with years of university education himself, had less trouble with this than I had at first. It was becoming clear to me that one did not need to go to university. I had to balance this with the true knowledge that Ian was a child with a great mind. I had yet to learn that great minds were the things that made for great leaders in the dance world.

I was certainly getting to know my son better. I was so grateful.

SEVENTEEN

No Other Schools

Once you make a decision,
the universe conspires to make it happen.
–Ralph Waldo Emerson

"Don't be sad if they don't accept you back at the end of summer school," said the words on the e-mail Ian was showing me on the computer screen. "They have the stupidest reasons for not wanting you!"

The e-mail had arrived a little more than a month before he was to return to the National Ballet School for another four-week summer school audition. It was from a former NBS classmate who had been reaccepted the year Ian had been home. Just that week, though, her parents had received the dreaded phone call and, as with many of her classmates, she would not be there when Ian returned to Toronto for summer school. Indeed, few of his original classmates would be there still–a situation that I was beginning to see would become increasingly familiar. On more than one occasion over the years, I'd meet people who knew someone (always a girl) who had been there for only a year; all a bit unsettling for a mother.

Ian was, however, so sure of himself. But, as older parents with years of life experience between us, Art and I knew that anything could and often did happen. This sentiment we chose not to express to Ian.

About the same time that Ian shared the e-mail with me, the National Ballet of Canada made a rare trek to the east coast on tour. Naturally we bought three tickets. It also happened that a very good friend of ours shared a mutual friend with Karen Kain, retired NBoC prima ballerina and now the ballet company's artistic associate, a role about which I knew nothing. This mutual friend of a friend was a local arts philanthropist extraordinaire and the reason that the National Ballet could even afford to go on an Easter tour this year, or so we were told. Because of this slightly-less-than-six degrees of separation, we had been invited to the after-party that was to be held in the donor's stunning downtown home. Art and I were looking forward to the evening almost as much as Ian. There was still enough of the Gloria Glamont in me to delight in the prospect of dressing up for an elegant soirée.

It seemed as if everyone who had even the slightest connection to the dance world in our little province had shown up for the performance that evening. Performing on stage at the Dalhousie Arts Centre, these professional dancers graced the very same stage on which we had seen Ian first dance; it was the place where we had discovered the startling truth that our boy was a dancer.

The ballet on offer that evening was a mixed program of short pieces, memorable for me in a slightly negative light: it was done on an almost bare stage, nothing at all like our *Nutcracker* experience in Toronto. Where were the beautiful sets? The orchestra? The visuals? As a visual person myself, the experience was diminished by these omissions. Soon I was to learn that for a ballet company to travel with full sets and costumes, let alone orchestra, was prohibitively expensive. I couldn't help but feel a bit sad. Outside major metropolises–home turf of major ballet companies–we felt we were somehow being deprived. We would never have that full experience. It was like a chocolate cake without icing–still delicious, but devoured with the vain realization that something was missing. I was one of the lucky ones, though. I had the means to travel to other places to get that icing on my chocolate cake. Others were not so fortunate. Yet, the evening did have its share of elegance and drama.

We arrived at a grand imposing house and noticed seemingly-unobtrusive security guards milling on the periphery. The guests milled about the grand foyer, all wonderfully attired as the audience members often are for a ballet after-party at the home of a major patron. Finally there were dancers. We made our way in and managed to snag a couple of glasses of wine from a passing waiter. It seemed as if everyone was anticipating the dancers' arrival. As we waited I noticed a strikingly beautiful and familiar-looking woman. Riveted by her elegance and a sense that I knew her, I could hardly take my eyes off her. Dressed in chic black, Karen Kain turned and smiled at us. I wondered how many of these shindigs she had been required to attend throughout her long and storied career in the performing arts. It seemed to me that it went with the territory. Gracious was the only word that came to mind. Perhaps she really was as nice as she always seemed when we heard her speak.

She nodded and said hello then turned toward Ian and smiled in recognition. "*You*, I remember," she said. Ian was thrilled since the only times she would have seen him was during *Nutcracker* rehearsals the previous Christmas season. And she seemed to somehow still remember him. It was a lovely memory that would stay with the mother in me for many years as we learned to navigate ever so carefully the edges of the ballet world.

We then made our way from the foyer into the exquisite, traditionally decorated living room. We could still see the front door and the staircase and when the dancers arrived. Immediately they made their way downstairs to the special buffet set up for them. I had no idea that, traditionally, what dancers do after performances is to eat and eat and eat.

Finally some of them, the men at least, began to make their way back up to where the guests waited to meet and congratulate them. There was no doubt that being able to hobnob with the patrons was prerequisite for a ballet dancer in today's world; it is what keeps ballet companies afloat.

Ryan Bourne, a 29-year-old principal dancer who looked 21 at the time, came over to chat. Dressed all in black, from the impeccable suit to the open-necked shirt, he was a handsome young man. I was struck by how much bigger and more imposing the men seemed when they were on stage. If I thought that the men looked grander on stage, I was certainly surprised at how tiny most of the female dancers were off-stage.

He and Ian, now all of thirteen years old, struck up a conversation. Ian told Ryan about his experience at the NBS and his plans to attend the four-week audition again for the upcoming summer.

"I know this sounds like blasphemy," Ryan said, "but there are other schools." From what I had read, Ryan had graduated from Quinte Ballet School in Belleville, Ontario, having had an experience of his own at the NBS. It's funny how you get the messages you need just when you need them: we all needed to hear this from someone like Ryan. It was the kind of thing that kept us grounded. But for Ian, there was no other school; he had made that abundantly clear to us. The Royal Winnipeg Ballet School had also extended to him an invitation to attend since he had appeared for the audition with his friend Freddy. In spite of the fact that he told them up front that he had already received an offer for summer school from NBS and was there for the audition experience, they decided to take a chance that his decision that NBS was the school for him might not be so final, and offered him an opportunity to go there as well. It was clear to me that Ian never even entertained the notion. (I had heard that the school in Winnipeg was giving male dancers free tuition in an effort to entice them–something that might not entice the students, but for the parents it might be a different story!) We knew that in the end it had to be Ian's choice. As parents Art and I were not going to push our own agenda. It turned out that we didn't have the luxury of remarking on such things for many years to come.

A few months later Ian was off to Toronto again–this time certain that this was his path. I was perhaps a bit more certain than I had been two years earlier, but he was still only thirteen years old.

Again we waited until the end of the first week to hear from him–a school policy that seemed to me a bit more sensible now that I'd had a year of being a National Ballet School parent. Things were going well, he said. It was only ten days into the four-week audition this time, but already the auditioning students had begun to tense up about pending decisions.

"I think they've already made up their minds," said Ian one evening when he called home the middle of the second week. "They've already been to our class three times!" The 'they' to whom he referred were Mavis Staines and Carole Chadwick who would again make the decisions.

It was at that moment that I started to relax about the whole thing. I knew that I needed to let it go, so I did. The fact that this was not my life but Ian's didn't diminish the auditioning decision's significance. I was beginning to have the first real inklings that it was not my life, but as one of his parents I knew it was our responsibility to guide him and be vigilant in our quest to assist him on whatever path he was supposed to take.

Monday, June 22

The call finally comes. It is from the National Ballet School registrar. She tells me that we are being asked to meet with the artistic director when we arrive in Toronto to meet Ian at the end of the audition period. I so want her to say that he has been invited back; I want her to be direct about it. But true to NBS form, she is vague to the end. I sigh. We have learned our lesson about never making assumptions about anything.

"I was just asked by Carole Chadwick to set up an interview with you," she says. "I don't really know what it's for." What B-S! I think.

The kids know.

"Did you get a call?" says Ian, calling several hours later. "No one got a call yet," he says.

I try to be a bit cagey. "I did," I say quietly.

He's elated. But his other friends from Halifax do not get calls.

It's always difficult when your child is the one who is picked and the others are not. Barb, Ian's teacher from Halifax who kept in touch, let us know that Ian's friends who were also auditioning had not been invited to attend. From what I'd heard about ballet parents, we were not normal in this way: we did not want to wave our child's success in the faces of those whose dreams had been dashed. But more about that later...

We just wished that the NBS would come right out and say things from the start. Perhaps a bit more transparency would have been a good thing.

August 3

They finally say all the things we need to hear.

Miss Staines welcomes us warmly into her office, bids us to take a seat and comes straight to the point (thank God!), "We watched him the first day and had to pinch ourselves. Is this for real, we asked, or is it just a one-time thing? And then the next day, and the next...of course you know why you're here today. We'd like to have Ian back."

She seems genuinely delighted (and even a bit surprised) at the extent of his development. So, we set off again to buy school uniforms.

This time, when Ian sees himself in the NBS uniform reflected in the store mirror a small smile begins to creep across his face. "It feels good," he says. "So different from two years ago."

And so it was. He returned to the school in September and his increasingly less frequent phone calls told us that he was revelling in his rediscovered freedom, freedom that he was now mature enough to appreciate. About six weeks after Ian had returned to Toronto, I opened my e-mail one morning to find a note from a fellow board member at the Maritime Conservatory. A singer by background himself, Neil mentioned Ian. "I'm sure you miss Ian...so young to leave home. Thankfully, you cared enough about him to let him go." Amen!

EIGHTEEN

Helicopters and Other Strangers

*A helicopter parent is a term for a person who
pays extremely close attention to his or her child or children,
particularly at educational institutions.
They rush to prevent any harm or failure from befalling them
or letting them learn from their own mistakes,
sometimes even contrary to the children's wishes.
They are so named because, like a helicopter,
they hover closely overhead, rarely out of reach
whether their children need them or not.*
–Wikipedia

In the grand scheme of things, there are ups and downs to everything–were it not for the rain, we would never truly appreciate the sunshine. Yet, day after day of sunshine might become monotonous. That's how it went as a ballet mom, particularly as an NBS mom. There were things about that school that I would eventually have to give up trying to understand. In the meantime, it was clear that it was in my own best interest to get into the school rhythm.

Each year began with what had become my traditional Labour Day activity–the trip to Toronto to take Ian back and get him settled at school. We developed a kind of ritual for that early September holiday: Art would drive us to the airport and hug Ian goodbye at the entrance to the security line. I'd fly with Ian to Toronto. We'd stay at our favourite Marriott Hotel where staff were getting to know us and where we were beginning to love each of them. Since we always arrived in the early evening, we'd have room service and watch a movie. Next morning we'd board a taxi to residence where Ian would be one of the first to arrive so he could get the pick of the beds in the room–two, three or even five to a room in the boys' residence. There was always one bed that was more prized. I'd help him unpack and lovingly put sheets on his bed and help him organize his dresser. (Although I realized that this was an exercise in futility, it was part of the annual mom ritual.) Then we'd go shopping for those school supplies that had been too heavy to pack, and have lunch at increasingly chi-chi restaurants. (In later years *Sassafraz* in Yorkville was his dining option of choice.) Then I'd go back to residence with him where the staff would call the airport limousine service for me and I'd fly home. Art, who would have stayed at home with the dog to luxuriate in one day of freedom to enjoy his beautiful house in peace, would pick me up. We'd take a deep breath and realize that as much as we would miss our son, we had freedom! Perhaps our advanced ages had something to do with the speed at which we were able to adapt. Perhaps that characteristic in itself saved us from hovering too much. In fact, as time went on, I loathed the thought of becoming a hoverer. And there were other parts of the rhythm of the school year that allowed us to make certain comparisons between ourselves and other parents.

For example, Parents' Day in early December of each year became one of my favourite rituals. I never really understood my own reaction to this, but after Ian's first year at the school, I eagerly looked forward to this annual pilgrimage. It was less to fulfil my diminishing need to have a finger in every aspect of my child's life and rather more because I enjoyed the feeling of the school, the palpable passion of the faculty and staff, and the peculiar intensity of the parents. These observations of parenting, both at the school and outside, helped me to see both similarities and differences between me and other moms and dads. All of these played a part in who I was becoming.

Other ballet parents, as well as parents whose kids were more likely to be in hockey or soccer than ballet, have given me food for thought over the years. When I was introduced to the term 'helicopter parent' some years ago, it was in relation to my position as a university professor. I had observed personally that the freshman students were becoming less and less self-reliant; more and more immature. I was experiencing something that I'd not seen before: parents were often the ones calling on behalf of their children (I wouldn't normally use this term to describe university students, but in this case it fits), appearing in the office and generally making a nuisance of themselves. These were the hoverers, and I shouldn't have been surprised for it was bound to happen. You see, these were the parents who began to put those ubiquitous 'Baby on Board' stickers on their cars twenty or so years ago.

In a 2006 *Washington Post* interview, a State University of New York anthropology professor suggested that these stickers were less a safety flag than a badge of accomplishment. "Look at me over here," they seem to be saying, "I'm a parent." I certainly had to agree with this conclusion the first time I saw one on the rear end of a black Porsche. Just precisely where was the baby anyway? These young parents with babies on board are largely the ones who so often seemed to become those helicopter parents. It was this generation of hovering moms and dads that were the parents of Ian's contemporaries. If anyone had suggested to us that we ought to have one of those cute stickers on our car windows we would have run away screaming in horror. We weren't that kind of parent. Or were we?

Well, if I'm really honest and scrutinize my life as a mom closely, I have to say I was on the edge. I had the potential. Art was my saving grace during Ian's early years. It was his grounding of an older, more experienced dad that helped me to avoid falling into the abyss of the over-protective mother. It would have been so hard to crawl out of it. Being a helicopter parent when your child is away at school is exhausting anyway. I learned that during Ian's first stint at NBS, and it became ever more apparent upon his return. But the parents of the day did give me pause for thought from time to time.

The first such encounter came during a fund-raiser for the local hospital research foundation that Art and I attended in Halifax. We were having a glass of wine and chatting with some doctors and their significant others that included Kathy, one of Art's young female partners, her physician husband, and another couple whom we had not met before. Kathy introduced us, and we discovered that the other woman was also a doctor. She worked part time as a civilian doctor with the armed forces and spent the rest of her time with her several children. I seem to remember that she had three–a noble and laudable task in itself. I marvelled at anyone who had that many children and still seemed reasonably together.

Kathy proceeded excitedly to tell this other woman that Art's and my son was at the National Ballet School, a revelation that always led to incredulity of one sort or another. The recipient of such information generally widens his or her eyes in a way that makes me wonder what's going on in their heads. This one wasn't going to keep me in suspense for long, though. She, too, widened her eyes and then moved almost imperceptibly into my personal space; slightly menacingly.

"*How* could you let your child go away to school? *I* could never do such a thing!"

I wasn't sure how I might have handled this during the early months of Ian's tenure at NBS, but this time it was different. And more importantly at this juncture, *I* was different.

I straightened up, did not back away and said very directly. "I let my son go away to school to pursue his dream because I love *my* child." It was as simple as that.

She backed down immediately. It was clear that she was one of those hovering parents who had to be there every minute. I also knew that within that particular social circle, what the parents wanted for the child often took precedence over what the child wanted–should the child ever be allowed an independent thought.

Most often, when told that I have a son at the National Ballet School, other parents are just curious. They ask dozens of questions about the school itself, but even more about how my son got started in ballet. Then they want to know what it's like there and often how much it costs. One of my colleagues at the university was moaning one day about how much his son's hockey activities cost him the year before. When I told him how much elite ballet schools cost in direct and indirect costs, he gasped and told me that he would be forever humble in my presence.

Then there are the other ballet moms themselves. They fall into two categories: the recreational ballet moms who dream their children will move them into the second group, the elite ballet moms–two different birds entirely. In fact, you might think that the ones who would be more difficult to get along with would be the moms of other elite ballet students. You'd be dead wrong. It seems as if those parents whose kids are not on the top are always the divas.

One of my first experiences with odd behaviour in ballet moms came one summer after Ian had been back at the NBS for two years. He was taking a summer dance intensive for two weeks at his old school, the same kind of program that had ignited his passion after his unceremonious dumping from NBS at the end of his first year. This time the teacher was a female dancer who had been a principal somewhere in Russia and was now with the artistic staff of a regional company in Canada.

I had arrived that afternoon to pick him up after class—it was still years before the driver's license. The class was taking place in the Conservatory's large auditorium that had a space for dance in front of the very small stage. It's true that I like to see Ian dance no matter what and no matter where, and given the opportunity to be a fly on the wall, I'll always take it. That day I stood at the very back just outside the auditorium doors, just far enough away not to be seen by the dancers–especially Ian. But I wasn't the only mom who had taken this vantage point. I was joined by another and I had much to reflect upon later when I got home to my journal.

August 5, 2003

It's noon. I'm standing outside the recital hall waiting for the class to end. Another mother whom I've never met (oh hell, maybe I have, I just didn't notice) is waiting. I strike up a conversation with her. (My first mistake.)

"The instructor looks younger than I thought she'd be from Barb's description," I say innocently enough.

"She's probably younger than she looks," says the mom.

I turn to look at the mom — 40 or 45, I think (maybe younger than she looks), blonde, rumpled crop pants (will this style never end?), shoulder-length non-descript hair, obviously overweight.

"Oh, maybe," I say. "Dancers often look older."

"She's anorexic," says the mom matter-of-factly. No question, no conversation, just a statement.

I look at the teacher from afar. She looks just like a ballerina to me. "Maybe she's just genetically slender," I say.

"No," says the other mother definitively. "She's anorexic. I can see it in the front of her legs."

Before I have a chance to get into an unwelcome argument, she's off on another subject.

"Oh," says the mom with slight alarm or so it seems to me, "there's a boy in the class."

I think for a moment I'll just let her take off on that subject but it seems cruel so I spare her. "Yes," I say, "he's my son. He's a student at the National Ballet School; he's home for the summer." This is my second mistake.

She asks about the NBS and tells me she could never send her child away to school. Not another one, I think. I grit my teeth. "Of course you could. If she had the passion and the talent."

Fortunately she's not listening to me anyway. "I know I probably shouldn't ask, but does your son have any problems with his sexual identity?"

I turn toward her. Have I heard her correctly? Did this person whom I have never met before and who has never been any closer to Ian than she is now actually ask such a personal question? I'm thrown a bit off balance by this out-of-the-blue comment from someone who has never even met Ian. But I'm not to be put off.

I laugh. "Ian? No, he knows exactly who he is." Not that it's any of her business, mind you. Why am I even answering?

Then the zinger. "Don't you worry about him up there around gay men? That he'll be influenced?"

Huh??

I cannot believe my ears. All I can think is "homophobe" and I'm not really sure where she's going with this line of conversation, if you can call it that. Instead of voicing this, I say, "I think he's as safe there as playing hockey or as an altar boy. Besides, either you're gay or you're not."

She is adamant. "No, you're not and I'm a physician."

That's supposed to make it better, or more acceptable, or even more polite? More authoritative? It seems to me to be worse coming from a helping professional.

In retrospect, I realized that I should have asked her then and there what her religious affiliation was because I have found over the years that this can explain a lot of prejudices. Then I should have asked her directly if she really thought that being gay was contagious. The very idea that someone, especially a physician, could hold such an outrageous belief was incomprehensible. The fact that she seemed to think that being a doctor, first, gave her the right to ask and second to make such ludicrous statements was beyond belief. As with many such encounters, we often think of the right response some time later, when it's too late. I had looked at her daughter in there dancing with the class. When she asked me about Ian's sexual orientation problems or lack thereof, I should have immediately asked her if her (clearly overweight) daughter had any problems pushing herself away from the doughnuts. Well, perhaps that wouldn't have been kind, but...

Throughout my career as a ballet mom, and especially when Ian returned to the National Ballet School, I noticed that if stage mothers have a certain reputation, then so too do ballet moms. I've come to the conclusion that there are three distinct camps into which these specimens fall:

1   The Harried Hoverers
2   The Dangerously Deranged
3   The Committed Careerists

From what I've observed, harried hoverers populate most of the recreational and regional ballet schools throughout North America. Magazines for dance teachers even write articles about them–although they have not yet picked up on my colourful label. I can't say for sure whether or not this reflects a general approach to parenting, but let's just say that it seems to be on the increase. A variation of helicopter parents, perhaps?

I came to know the Harried Hoverers during the parents' meetings fairly early in the game. It seemed to me that the very fact that the NBS had initiated such parents' meetings after so long in business was a testimony to the general increase in hovering. Art and I dutifully attended these meetings, first for the content they might provide and later for the sheer entertainment value. You could pick out the hoverers as they took their seats in the theatre where all the meetings were held. They sat on the edges of their seats, their notebooks open and pens poised, leaning slightly forward as if to avoid missing even a syllable that might emanate from the mouths of the artistic director, the academic principal and the head of residence, all of whom were always lined up behind a table on the theatre's stage.

"What do you suppose they're taking notes about?" I asked Art on more than one occasion. I never did have the cheek to ask any of them. One thing I did know for sure: there seemed to be a negative correlation between the number of questions a parent asked (especially about reacceptance procedures) and the likelihood of the offspring's being reaccepted to the school. In other words the more a parent hovered, the less likely it was that the child was a seriously gifted dancer–with a few notable exceptions!

One Parents' Day, the discussion revolved around the possibility of creating a support group for parents. All I could think of was that they were probably right. Some of them did need counselling more than did their children. I have no doubt that, over the years, the school thought that Art and I belonged in that group!

In addition to the many questions raised in public about the unloved reacceptance procedures with which we had had first-hand in-your-face experience, there were other odd obsessions. One of them was food. Parents with young children in residence were evidently infatuated by the food issue. It was inevitable that the subject would come up. Indeed, it was always worth a giggle and when the topic did not surface, I was actually disappointed.

On one such occasion, a hand close to the front shot up. (I'm sure she had a notebook open on her lap.) She had a question for Janet, the wonderful head of the NBS residence who always had the time to listen to even the most distraught and foolish among us. I had personal experience of falling into the latter category, I'm afraid.

"I was wondering," began the mother, "what the residence is doing about the issue of students who are vegetarians." She then related to all of us that her daughter was a vegetarian and was now forced to eat all kinds of food and was gaining weight. This dietary fact about the student came as a complete surprise to Janet who said that the child had never mentioned that she was a vegetarian and was happily eating anything that the school offered. The truth seemed to be that the mom was a vegetarian, a lifestyle that clearly had not been embraced wholeheartedly by her daughter. Indeed, according to Janet, in cases of those who did declare themselves vegetarian, their vegetable of choice was the French fry.

The hoverers among us had a couple of directions in which to go. They could evolve into those Committed Careerists I began to notice among the more successful of Ian's classmates over the years; or they could go the direction of the Dangerously Deranged; and these DDs were on a continuum if ever I saw one.

My experience with the DD's was on the lower end of the continuum where the ballet moms' derangement had yet to progress into full-blown cases, dangerously close to insanity. I remember discussing the National Ballet School with the mother of a young dancer who had not been accepted into its full-time program. To say that she herself was bitter would be an understatement. According to her, the school had decided not to admit her daughter only because of her body type. Evidently she was too small or something of that ilk. But rumour had it that this mom had torn a strip off the artistic staff, venting her rage about her daughter's short-changed career as she saw it. I didn't witness this personally, but it wasn't much of a stretch to picture it after our conversation.

I've only read about those ballet moms who are full-blown cases of dangerous derangement. Around the time that Ian returned to the NBS, a story made the news about one such mom. According to the reports, this mom had cheated welfare out of $15,000 to send her daughter to an elite ballet school in Europe. Her belief that her 22-year-old daughter was entitled to the best ballet education she could get caused the judge in her case to suggest that she was funding "…what many would regard as an extravagance." When I read that, I wasn't sure who was more wrong-headed: the mom or the judge.

Ballet moms, though, had nothing on the tennis dad whose antics were reported in the newspapers in early 2006. It seems that the father of two young tennis players in France had stooped to drugging his kids' opponents. He reportedly said that he felt so much anguish and panic over the need to see them win matches that he had lost his reason. Indeed! I suppose parents of intensely focused kids face many of the same problems. Only a few resort to such drastic and, in his case, lethal methods.

As my own career as a ballet mom progressed, I saw a lot of committed careerists. These committed, but not over-involved, parents were the ones who went out of their way emotionally, financially and physically to support their children's dreams. They tried to be realistic about talent and potential and provided those kids with whatever they could muster. Whenever I've read anything over the years about gifted children who grew up to be truly gifted contributors to society, whether as musicians, artists, dancers, scientists, athletes, etc. they all had a couple of things in common. The most surprising one was not talent or drive. Many of us have that. They had a combination that included someone in their lives who supported, nurtured and mentored their talent. Often it was a parent but when parents were not supportive, those geniuses found other mentors. Even Mozart, as prodigious as he was, would likely not have given his music to the world and developed into the adult genius, albeit short-lived, if not for his father.

I read a story about American Ballet Theater's principal dancer Ethan Steiffel's parents. They would drive him two hours each way so that he could take ballet classes at the Milwaukee Ballet School, then four hours to Chicago so that he could perform in *Nutcracker*, all before he was fourteen.

Maybe the sages who write about helicopter parents have it wrong after all. Perhaps the helicopters are the ones whose blades rotate faster than others so that they can provide lift to their children; that's the kind of helicopter parent I want to be.

158

NINETEEN

If Only They Were Orphans

Parents are as central to the life of the National Ballet School
as they are to the lives of their children.
–NBS Parents' Handbook

Mavis Staines once told the parents' group at a meeting in the school theatre that she was often asked by others outside the school about the public stereotype of the horrors of working with so many ballet parents. I could just picture the conversation:

"So, tell us, Ms. Staines, how awful is it to have to deal with the students' parents?"

The stereotypical image of the ballet parents and the ballet mom, in particular, is bad enough: parents of elite ballet students must be just short of demonic or so the rumour goes. Mavis told us that she always informed the inquirers that the horrors were, in fact, a myth. She was even quoted in an article for dance teachers saying, "…The myth of the ballet mom is truly just a myth from my perspective…" She really enjoyed the parents. I believed her then and I still believe her. One of the reasons is because students at elite ballet schools hound their parents to not get involved.

As Ian and his classmates liked to say, Mavis held their very futures in her hands. It was so very true. I learned early on that if Ian called with a problem, my first inclination to jump in with both feet to intervene had to be stopped in its tracks. I learned to ask the simple question: "Would you like us to do anything?" (I always included Art in this since he, like most men, is focused on solutions, not talking about issues!) More than 99% of the time, the answer to the question was, "No, do nothing. I just wanted you to know."

Thus, we parents became a relatively silent bunch except when it came to complaining about security at the residence or carrot sticks during snack times. From time to time, things seemed to hearken back to earlier eras in the evolution of ballet schools, and it was clear to us that the school's most fervent wish was likely "...if only they were orphans."

I had heard stories about the history of the ballet schools and that the students had been chosen from orphanages. A few mouse clicks later, and I found it to be true.   The modern elite ballet schools like the National Ballet School in Canada, the Royal Ballet School in London and the School of American Ballet in New York share a common history with the establishment of the first such residential school in St. Petersburg, Russia. Empress Anna Ioannova decreed on May 4, 1738 that French ballet Master Jean-Baptiste Landé should establish the Imperial Theatre School. I can imagine his pondering at length how he might go about doing this. One of the first things he must have considered was where he would find students. This was a new thing. He couldn't do what modern elite schools do, and embark on national and international tours to audition potential students from city to city or by collecting DVDs. So, who would come to his school?

As I read about this historic new approach to arts education, I wondered who came up with the idea of where to find the students. Was it Landé himself? The empress? The janitor, perhaps? The solution to the quandary, though, had interesting implications that resonated through the centuries. He chose twelve boys and twelve girls who were orphans of palace servants. Talent or passion seemed of little consideration; only availability and, presumably, enough athletic potential to survive the training. The bonus had to be no parents! There would be no one to wonder about lights-out times or dining facilities or even whether or not the little one was to be reaccepted for continuing training. What bliss it must have been for the artistic staff.

The trend continued with Catherine the Great's desire to establish a theatre arts school in Moscow in 1773. Its first students were the orphans of civil servants. Even if Canada's National Ballet School's artistic director in the 21st century personally didn't think that ballet parents were a problem, it was clear to me from reading the odd article in ballet magazines that others didn't share her view.

I once read an article titled "My Daughter is a Diva" wherein the author pens a how-to article directed at dance teachers with the purpose of helping them to deal with those pesky parents. One of the most interesting recommendations she had was to limit the parents' opportunities to chat with one another. Evidently, according to this particular dance teacher, such chatter can lead to gossip which, as we all are supposed know, can lead to competitive banter. Presumably this would be something along the lines of, "My daughter's arms are better than your daughter's," or perhaps, "Your daughter's having a bit of a weight challenge these days." In fact she suggested that there be a no-talking-at-all policy in the waiting areas. Yikes! I guess that's why a residential school is so wonderful for teachers. The parents live so far from one another, there's hardly any chance to gossip for any length of time. E-mail, however, is gradually changing that.

It seems that if it hadn't been for the pushy ballet mom who was the particular gift to one young dancer called Peggy, she might not have emerged into the world years later as Margot Fonteyn, arguably one of the best ballerinas of all time. Apparently her mom Nita Hookham dragged her from one teacher to another until she finally found one they liked–Ninette de Valois at the Royal Ballet.

Involved ballet moms seem to have a long and distinguished pedigree. Truth be told, we moms do play an integral part in the development of the child as a person. We are not the experts. I mean this, even if parents are former dancers themselves: parents have a whole other set of problems to deal with. Although the school took steps to enhance communication with parents in a formal way, there were subtleties of a more insidious nature that, when interpreted from the perspective of the peripheral parents, came back to the realization that it would be easier for them if the kids were orphans.

One day during the winter semester after Ian returned to the

National Ballet School, he called to chat–an increasingly less common occurrence as he began to find his own voice.

"Oh, by the way, Mom," he said in passing, "Did I tell you about *Tristan and Isolde*?"

No, he had not and I had only the slightest recollection of his mentioning this new production that the National Ballet of Canada was embarking on.

"The casting list goes up this week."

Casting list? I thought.

"There's a lot of talk around res, one way and another." ('Res'—short for 'residence.')

He continued. "You know you can't be in Music Night if you're in the ballet."

I did seem to remember something about this. Indeed, Music Night was another of the annual highlights of the school year for us parents. When I thought about it, I remembered putting it out of my mind, hoping it would go away. I always wanted Ian to have every opportunity but, selfishly, I didn't want to miss seeing Music Night although it conjured more complications than I cared to think about.

"Some people say they'll be devastated if they're not cast."

It occurred to me that no one (Read: 'parents') ever seemed to know how many parts there would be or of what gender, what age and (need I say it?) what height.

"Some people don't want to miss Music Night." He didn't offer whether or not he fell into this category. Music Night was also a highlight for Ian, since he was looking forward to being one of the vocal soloists with his own moment on stage in the spotlight this year.

He continued, "I figure it's a win-win situation, though. Either way I'll be happy."

Wow! What a kid, I thought to myself. We taught him well.

While I was still patting myself on the back, I stopped abruptly. Wait a minute. What about rehearsals? When would they be? The show was scheduled early in May and spring break was in April. We had airline tickets booked. The kids needed a holiday. Hell, we needed a holiday. Now I would have something to worry about until the list went up. The notion of inquiring about this hadn't even entered my mind. It would be pointless and embarrassing for all– including, and perhaps most of all, for Ian. I knew that I'd really have to learn to detach myself even more since I had no control whatsoever.

Thursday, January 30

The words a long-distance mother never wants to hear at the other end of the phone.

"Mom, I'm sick,"

Vomiting. A bit of diarrhea. A dozen other students in residence sick, including one room-mate.

But–he doesn't sound too forlorn. I listen very closely for any sign that he's really missing Mom. He doesn't seem to be, but I worry anyway. I think I'm allowed.

Ian in the midst of an update on the state of his stomach says, "By the way…" Don't I sit up straighter every time I hear those three words? I never know what's coming next. "By the way, you won't be seeing me in Music Night." He's been cast in the ballet.

What will this mean, I wonder.

Of course, we didn't get to Music Night that year. We went to see *Tristan and Isolde* instead. It was an odd ballet, but we enjoyed seeing Ian up there on stage with professional dancers in a large production. It was just one lesson in realizing that when it came to some issues, he might as well be an orphan.

Another rather smaller but infinitely more important issue arose some time later. Until then, mailings from the school had been addressed to us by name. These mailings included annual reacceptance letters, report cards, memos regarding upcoming events and the like. One day I picked up the mail and thumbed through. Seeing the now familiar logo of the National Ballet School, I picked out the envelope and glanced down at the address label.

Rather than being addressed to 'Dr. and Mrs. Parsons' as it had been in the past, now it was addressed to 'Parents/Guardians of Ian Parsons'. What? I thought. Did we lose our identities? It seemed a small thing, but it was meaningful. It's something a school does unthinkingly, not knowing how such a small action is interpreted within the framework in which we operate on a regular basis. Years later when it came up in a discussion with a group of other parents, it was evident that we had not been the only ones who had noted this subtle, if unintended, snub. Even after those discussions, all correspondence not sent to us from the foundation–the fundraising arm which always seemed to know we were individuals with names–came to 'Parents/guardians of…' If only they truly had been orphans!

One of the things few people know about elite ballet schools is that the student has to be reaccepted every year. Just as in that first year when we awaited 'the call' or 'no call', we went through the same purgatory every spring thereafter. During that week in May when the calls would be made, we would wait. It never came. We didn't stop worrying until Ian was about two years from graduation. It was then that we realized that he had what they wanted and nothing except a major injury or his changing his mind would result in his rejection by the school. Years later Ian would tell us that he himself never really worried after he went back the second time. We realized that the waiting for the call was just another of the parent things that we had to experience.

We couldn't help but feel that the NBS often had us by the throat. Exchange planning was another issue.

Every year the students who were in the senior school would get letters indicating that they were eligible to go on summer exchange. When Ian was in Grade 10 he was eligible for a summer exchange, so we parents knew it was likely that he'd spend his mandatory summer school session not in Toronto but in some foreign country— the school had partner schools in the US, UK, France, Germany and Australia, in the main. We didn't have any input.

March 19, 2005

They have us by the throat again. Two weeks ago Ian calls. "Mom and Dad, guess where I'm going on exchange this summer?" We can't guess. "Cannes." We laugh. We have long teased him that he would likely end up in France since he dropped his French classes this year. The prospect of a summer holiday on the French Riviera is terrific. We spend a week doing some research so that we can meet him at the end of summer school and do a bit of touring.

Then, another call. "Miss Hess stopped me in the hall today," he says. "There are too many kids going to Cannes. So they've decided to send me to Stuttgart."

Stuttgart? Who goes there we think. We have no idea. Art and I chat and decide unanimously that Germany isn't nearly as appealing to us as a place to spend a bit of time this summer. Oh, well.

Then a week later, another call comes. "Brace yourself," Ian begins. "I'm going to Seattle."

It seems that "they" talked to his ballet teacher who allegedly pronounced that he didn't want to risk an injury in such a strenuous program as Stuttgart was meant to be. (Evidently for older dancers? Who knows? Not us for sure, and no one it seems is telling.) So he's off to the Pacific Northwest Ballet School in Seattle. Ian has decided to be excited about it regardless of where they send him. We cannot do less–or be less.

We have so many questions. Why did they choose Ian as one of the students not to send to France? Is Stuttgart really so arduous? Do they ever lose students to the exchange schools? Why PNB? What's there? It's really clear to us that this information is strictly on a need-to-know basis. We are merely the parents. We do not need to know. We know there will never be answers that we'll understand.

I have mental whiplash from so many changes in my

thought process. We, too, buckle under to the NBS flow. We will be taking a summer vacation on the west coast of the USA.

And a terrific vacation it turned out to be! Thanks to the NBS decision, we decided to capitalize on it and flew to Seattle via Vancouver in early August to visit Ian during the final days of his summer school tenure in Seattle. Wow! The classes were enormous, quite unlike those we had seen in Canada. A chat with one or two American ballet parents gave us the feeling that they were even more intense about the whole thing than were we. One of Ian's classmates was a student at the School of American Ballet in New York.

"It's so much more competitive there," said his mother as we sat on the sidelines, watching the final class. I wondered if it *really* was that much more competitive or if that was just a parental perception. In any case, her son was auditioning for the New York City Ballet. We wished them well. (He did get a contract there a year or two later.)

We rented a car in Seattle and did the road trip down the coast to San Francisco. It was wonderful! The coast of Oregon and northern California was blanketed in fog so thick it was like driving in a vanilla milk shake most of the way, but every now and then it lifted long enough for the stunning view to come into focus. The wild Pacific wasn't that foreign to us Atlantic-coasters, but the place had a completely different feeling. Simply standing under magnificent redwoods in the amazing silence of the forest and gazing at the mists as they bounced off the rays of filtered sunlight made me feel just a little closer to heaven I think. There was no doubt in my mind at that point that I had come to terms with my role: I would always be his mom. My child was no orphan–but he didn't belong to me either. Maybe the NBS did know what it was doing after all. Yet, they had us right until the end.

May 31, 2007

It's never over, it seems–right to the bitter end. They'll try to get us even on graduation day! It's about the wine. Rumor

166

has it that in someone's wisdom (as always an unnamed individual) there should be no wine available to be imbibed by anyone at the dinner and dance following the graduation ceremony. A dinner without wine? No wine at the dance? Good Lord! The parents deserve at least one final crumb.

It occurs to us that we might be alone in our incredulity but after a little investigation, it seems we have company. Other parents have heard the news and they are not happy either.

"We're just going to bring our own bottle anyway," says Doris, mom of one of Ian's long-time friends and frequent room-mate.

And there are others who think that the school should come across with this one final indulgence.

So, here I go, writing an e-mail to the general powers that be since I'm not entirely sure who actually makes such decisions. I imagine they'll be glad (and relieved) to see our backsides in a month.

I did write the e-mail, this time to beg their indulgence for us. I suggested that for many of us such a once-in-a-lifetime event called for a celebratory glass of something other than apple juice. I never did know what the problem was or, indeed, who had the problem. All I know is that on graduation day there was wine at dinner and at the dance. No one got drunk–although many parents seemed sorely tempted–and no one underage drank anything, not so far as I could see. But at least that one last time the school powers took parents into consideration, and I thank them for that.

TWENTY

The Fourth Wall

The space separating the audience from the action
of a theatrical performance, traditionally conceived of
as an imaginary wall completing the enclosure of the stage.
–American Heritage Dictionary 4th edition

When Ian was a very little boy and we looked at the possibilities in his future as parents often do, it was increasingly clear that he would be a performer. We didn't really know where or what kind of performance, but we did realize that his desire and passion for being on stage in front of an audience would guide his choices. Like most parents of performing children, we adored seeing him on stage. Even in the National Ballet School's parents' handbook they acknowledged it: "...Seeing their child on stage is one of the greatest thrills for all parents." This is virtually an understatement for any ballet mom or dad. Performance was an important part of Ian's reason for dancing. As time went on Art and I often joked that, during times of child-induced stress which all parents experience from time to time, they ask of themselves the inevitable question, "Why do people have children, anyway?" We knew the answer: for entertainment, and we had entertainment in spades.

From that very first time when we saw Ian dance on stage at the age of nine to his final performance as a student at Canada's National Ballet School, we tried never to miss an opportunity to see him perform. We were very experienced at sitting on the other side of that fourth wall.

For six months running up to graduation, Art worked on a special

DVD for Ian. On long winter nights that year I could hear snippets of now-familiar music wafting from the office in the front of the house. Occasionally I'd hear a muttered profanity as the computer took on a life and direction of its own. The DVD Art was creating would be a compilation of all the dance-related videos we had managed to accumulate over the years—excerpting the early ones (who needs six minutes of a gaggle of eleven-year-olds?) and including later years' full-length performances. In this process, my job was to view everything and find Ian's performances buried deep inside the hours and hours of videos produced by his early dance schools for proud parents like us. So, I took the old VHS tapes to the family room and sat on the floor in front of the television alone reminiscing, often laughing, over performances we'd attended. My responsibility was to note exactly their places on the tapes. (Of course, sometimes I'd forget to reset the tape counter...) Then I'd return them to the office where Art was hard at work, busily transferring these old tapes to digital files and then painstakingly editing to produce a program Ian and the rest of us would be happy to watch. Whenever he told others that he was doing this, they marveled at his patience and his doing it for his son. Clear to me, it was a labour of love that took us down memory lane reliving those magic moments of sitting on the other side of the fourth wall. We were always proud parents sitting there in the audience, but as the years progressed and as both Ian's and the performances of his classmates became more and more technically advanced and artistically polished, it was even more of a thrill for us. Although we were clearly hooked on Ian's work, the experience opened our eyes to dance as pure entertainment, a novel notion to us.

Art and I might find ourselves at home flipping through the television channels before bed, desperately trying to find something to enjoy that required more than the IQ of a gnat, and then stumbling upon a ballet-related production. The flicking would inevitably stop and we would become entranced. One evening Art looked at me and said, "Can you believe us? It's not so many years ago that we would never even consider watching ballet on TV!" It was a testimony to our commitment to our child, and yet it was something more than that.

Ian's passion for ballet and our desire to understand something of his world led us to seek out more and more about this art form, so much so that in due course we became ballet patrons. Our role, however, was clearly as audience members and our son never let us forget that we didn't truly understand. That was okay with us. No matter how many ballet performances we watched, either on television or on great stages of the world–including Covent Garden in London–our greatest pleasure was sitting in the audience, watching our son.

The NBS offered several distinct annual performance opportunities. The first one of each year was the presentation for those who attended the school's annual general meeting in late November or early December. A day later, those who had come for parents' day saw a repeat of that performance. We never missed one. It consisted largely of a disparate collection of pieces, with little or no participation of the students in the junior grades. Indeed, we perceived a school idea that the first semester was not long enough to produce anything by the younger students worthy of public consumption. They were probably quite right, but in the early years we were not alone in our wishes that we could have seen our child perform more often. We did, however, come to appreciate the wisdom of this. At the end of the year, there would be a Junior School Closing presentation that included all the junior students. The pieces were very carefully choreographed to ensure that each and every student was capable of producing a creditable performance. No one would leave the theatre hinting that students at Canada's National Ballet School were not up to snuff, as it were.

Before the shows and at intermissions we often sat in the Betty Oliphant Theatre with our mouths clamped shut so we could look at and listen to parents around us–always interesting and often eye-opening.

In the spring of Ian's grade 10 year, we happily traveled to Toronto to see the Spring Showcase Performance, the *pièce de resistance* of the school's annual performance year where the senior students have a chance to shine. We were impressed by the entire cast as usual–especially with the one grade nine boy who admirably held his own among grade 11 and 12 boys and students of the NBS post-secondary intensive dance program. The others all had a leg up on him in years of training as well as sheer physical development. As an audience member, you would never have known. Ian danced the part of one of the athletes in the all-male ballet The Playing Field, a moving piece based on *Lord of the Flies*. You might recall from your high school English literature that the story is a slightly gruesome one–one that you might not think of as ballet fodder –involving a group of English schoolboys marooned on an island. A hierarchy emerges and groups splinter with the inevitable power struggle ensuing, leading even to the beating death of one of the characters. Ian was one of the beaters. There was no doubt in our minds his flair for the dramatic and his acting ability would stand him in good stead. That ballet took up almost half the production, while tutus, of course, populated the rest.

May 30, 2005

Sometimes I think I shouldn't have that second glass of wine before NBS performances. And sometimes I think I should have four! We are sitting in the audience before the curtain rises, perusing the program. The group of people in the row in front of us clearly consists of parents and friends of one or more of the students. One turns around, her finger pointing at a name in the program and then pointing to the woman sitting to her right. "Proud mother," she says beaming.

Maybe I'm just a bit too tight-assed, but I'd rather swallow glass than be so blatant about my personal pride. The truth is you'd never know who you were saying it to. We smile and nod. We say nothing.

Then the very well-heeled looking American woman sitting beside me (I only know that she is American because she tells me later) turns to me to strike up a conversation. She starts asking questions to find out if we too are parents (they

172

are) and what part our daughter is playing. We tell her which part our son is playing.

Maybe it's me, but I always seem to catch an "edge" from such exchanges with parents we don't know. It's as if they are trying to find out if our child has a bigger role than their child. Maybe I'm just too sensitive to this–but it does give us food for thought.

It seemed a long time coming, but finally Ian was cast for solo debut in the spring. He was in grade 11–one year before graduation. We had been in Mavis's office the day before to discuss Ian's future when she asked me if I was nervous for Ian's solo. I told her that I was not. Indeed, I was terribly excited, both for Ian and for us as his proud parents. However, at dinner just before the performance my stomach was churning. We sent Ian a good luck note and a pack of gum, a private joke among us three. (You don't say 'good luck' to a performer. In the dance world one wishes them *Merde*! If you don't speak French, you'll have to look that one up.) We took our seats in the front row of the balcony of the Betty O. I had the same feeling, sitting there waiting for the performance to begin, as I had all those years earlier when we sat awaiting his very first performance. Earlier I had asked Art if he thought we had a dancer on our hands, and he had replied, "Wait until I see him dance." This time we wondered quietly if we were crazy for even thinking that we might have a rising star on our hands. Just as with that first time, we'd know by the time this performance was over.

Former Artistic Director of the National Ballet of Canada, the illustrious choreographer James Kudelka, had chosen Ian as one of the dancers around whom he would create a new work to be premiered at Spring Showcase Performances. It consisted of a male solo, *a pas de deux,* and a female solo of what I would judge to be contemporary ballet. Called *Four Proverbs*, it was accompanied by original music created by attaching specific words to specific notes. Whenever a note was repeated, the sung word was repeated and resulted in an unusually perplexing vocal line. What can I say? It was artistic...

The lights came up just slightly. There, in the back left corner of the stage, was a young man's body silhouetted against the background. Clad in bright blue tights and ballet slippers and with only that millimetre of spandex between him and the audience, he began to move. As he moved into the light, I realized with a bit of a start that Ian was clearly no longer my little boy. He was a young man embarking on his path, a path destined by something greater than us. If ever I had had the slightest doubt that I as a mom or Art as his dad or Mavis Staines as his mentor had done the wrong thing, I knew at that moment that we had all been right.

I held my breath as he moved through what he had told us was a deceivingly difficult solo. He was spectacular. Then came his duet with his startlingly beautiful and talented partner Nadine Drouin, a year his senior at the school. They made a striking couple and gave a powerful performance. When it was all over, Art and I looked at each other in the dark. There was no doubt. He was a star in our minds already. We only hoped that we'd get a chance to see Nadine and Ian dance together again at some time in the future. (Several months later, Nadine was offered a contract as an apprentice with the National Ballet of Canada. We were so pleased for her. She deserved it.)

During the intermission, we wandered out to the balcony for a breath of air. Bob Sirman, then the administrative director at the school, was doing the same. He told us that he had been sitting with Dr. Meen, and when Ian's performance was over Dr. Meen had leaned over and said, "What have we wrought?" It seemed to be unanimous. But I wondered what Mavis Staines had thought of it. No doubt that would be most meaningful to Ian.

I didn't have long to wait to find out. After the performance, as we were walking through the front door of the school next door to wait for Ian, Mavis was coming in through the back. "You must be very proud of the performances this week," I said. There was no doubt that much of the success of these students was her doing either directly or indirectly.

"I was just about to say the same to you," she said. "Ian was wonderful. What a strong performance."

Just as she was asking us to convey this to Ian, he walked in and Art and I melted into the background so that she could tell him herself. When he told us about it later, he was beaming. Mavis had approved.

Art and I realized that for the rest of our lives, we'd be content to sit on the other side of the fourth wall.

TWENTY-ONE

A World Apart

*Stockholm Syndrome...in which a hostage begins to identify with
and grow sympathetic to his or her captor.*
–American Heritage Dictionary, 2nd ed

We're odd in a lot of ways, we human beings. Sometimes our mind-set is vulnerable to an idea that at other times might sound completely preposterous, and it's at those times of weakness that we can fall victim to the inner workings of our own minds. After a few years as NBS parents, appreciating all that the school had helped our child accomplish while at the same time stewing in our own powerlessness and periodic confusion, we were susceptible to odd ideas. It was during such a time of cognitive dissonance, some time during Ian's last year at the school, where these two sets of thoughts co-exist, that Art stumbled upon an article about Stockholm Syndrome. We were immediately and inexplicably drawn to the parallels between our child and the unfortunate individuals who suffer from this syndrome.

In 1973 a now-infamous situation occurred in Stockholm, Sweden. During six days in captivity, bank employees who had been captured by bank robbers began to show signs of loyalty to their captors. The term 'Stockholm Syndrome' was coined at the time by a criminologist and has ever after been loosely used to describe the relationship that can develop between captor and captive. The specific characteristics that are used to identify such individuals seemed to describe what we as parents frequently perceived about our children's relationship with an elite ballet school. It seemed that my own son, not to mention most of his classmates, often exhibited signs that they suffered from a genus of the disorder at least some of the time at the school.

First, for a diagnosis of Stockholm Syndrome, there has to be a perceived threat. Well, if facing possible ejection from your deepest passion isn't a threat, I don't know what is. On more than one occasion Ian told us that the students mostly feared the artistic director and the rest of their teachers. He, however much fear he might have experienced (and as a mom I cannot really know the answer to that), always said that he loved her. She was his mentor. Hmm...as I thought about the second characteristic of the syndrome, I wondered at the extent to which this also fit.

There has to be some element of kindness that the captive feels the captor is displaying. There is no argument about this. The NBS staff was for the most part thoughtful, caring and even sympathetic to the students. I doubt that many of today's kids would stay in a place for as long as these did were there no such kindnesses. Besides, if there were no kindnesses I believe school loyalty would be seriously diminished.

Another characteristic is that there has to be isolation from other perspectives. This could not be truer. The residential nature of such elite schools makes them perfect for creating a kind of mirrored wall around the students. When they look out, they see a reflection of themselves and the world of ballet, doubtless a world apart from everything else. Even for those children whose parents live in Toronto–thus they don't live in residence–the school day is so long and the requirement for parents' submission so strong that they, too, are subject to the same kind of isolation. I remember Ian saying that it was difficult to have friends who were not ballet dancers since no one else understood their intensity or dedication. For those who did not have this dedication, their tenure at the school was precarious. I often wondered how many there really were. As I thought more about this, it occurred to me that I might find some of them on the web, so I surfed.

Surfing, I found a blog that was penned by a former National

Ballet School student who summed up that dedication/isolation issue this way: "The hierarchy at NBS is simple: either you dance or you suck." I had thought this was the case, but this just confirmed my perception.

The final characteristic of the syndrome is the captives' feeling that there is no escape. I have often wondered if the kids believed they could get out. As I noted earlier, in Ian's first year at the NBS he had asked us how we'd feel if he proceeded through to graduation and then, for some reason, decided not to dance. Would we think that our money had been wasted? It was the kind of question that just seems to hit you out of the blue when you're least expecting it, especially coming from a thirteen-year-old boy. Then you realize that, of course, this is a perfectly reasonable consideration. He will mature into a different person. Our answer to that question would have considerable impact as to whether or not he was one who felt that there was no escape. This would be especially true of the kids who were dancing more for their parents than for themselves. The movie *Center Stage* captured this dramatically with the star student of the ballet school's possessing a fine ballet body and the ability to persevere through the training. In the end, when she was finally able to face the reality of her lack of passion in the face of a mother who was clearly more dedicated than was her daughter, she said to her ballet mom, "You didn't have the feet. I don't have the heart."

We had answered Ian from our hearts. No, we would not think our money was wasted nor would we be disappointed. By that time we had already figured out that a child has to do what a child is supposed to do, even if that meant changing direction along the way. He was visibly relieved at our response and it never came up again. Canada's National Ballet School would give him an education that would stand him in good stead no matter what he ultimately did with his life. As he proceeded through his training it was clear to us, though, that he had both the feet and the heart.

It truly was a different world these creatures inhabited. As beautiful, smart, dedicated and passionate as these teenagers were, one of the things that struck us most was the perfectionism rampant

179

among them. Not one seemed to realize how beautiful, smart, dedicated, talented and passionate they were. We were struck, too, by the extent to which they possessed a distinct inferiority complex about themselves and their training.

Canada's National Ballet School purports to be one of the premier schools in the world, training dancers who have gone on to grace the stages of the world at the highest levels of the art form. This is what their literature says, but more importantly it's what others outside the school say as well. It is probably one of the three best such schools in the world for a number of different reasons, only one of which is the outcomes.

It's also in the way that the school does what it does. It may not be what parents want. In fact, I came to the grudging awareness that a child who is gifted in this way presents peculiarities that the school understands in a way that parents never can. We tend to see our own children in one way; the school sees them differently. It views them through their unique frame of experience in guiding talented dancers toward their unique place in the world. We see our children through the prism of unconditional love.

But this understanding didn't explain that rampant feeling of inferiority that bubbled to the surface of so many of these gifted students–including the one I knew best. Why did the students often believe that they didn't measure up? We knew from long experience that this was an issue. But, Art and I liked to do our part in enlarging Ian's world, and I believe we tackled this conundrum as well as we could.

Spring break in grade 10 loomed. We decided that it was time Ian went to the city that his dad and I had visited nine months before his birth. So we booked airline tickets, show tickets and a hotel room and jetted off to New York City for six days to show him a world that he had not seen before.

We had bought tickets to see the Broadway musicals *Rent* and *Movin' Out;* the first Ian's request, the second something we thought he should see since it consisted entirely of dance pieces choreographed by Twyla Tharp to the music of Billy Joel. Twyla Tharp was for Ian; Billy Joel was for us. Ballet companies don't usually perform at that time of year; it's between seasons. We were disappointed. A bit of surfing, however, uncovered a single ballet performance. I was excited at first but then disappointment set in again. The American Ballet Theater's studio company's final performance of the run was at the Joyce Theater the evening we were to arrive. Airline travel being what it was, we didn't like to pay for tickets that a delayed flight might make useless. If we arrived in New York late, we'd have to forfeit them. As luck would have it, our flight did get in on time and after we checked into our hotel right on Times Square, we considered the possibility of last-minute tickets.

Art got on the phone and after several false starts managed to come up with three tickets for that night–front row, no less. We did wonder why these three tickets might still be available and were not among the most expensive. That night we found out.

The Joyce Theater is a wonderful dance performance space in New York's Soho district. A venue for the more artistic and experimental works, it also hosts smaller companies such as the ABT Studio company as well as visiting companies from other parts of the US and abroad. Ballet Jazz de Montreal performs there from time to time. It is an intimate setting, with small-scale amenities. It was a bit of a thrill, I must admit, to be there among the more dance-literate types in a world-class performing arts city. But our seats... They were, indeed, in the front row. At the Hummingbird Centre in Toronto, front-row seats meant one of the best views in the house; not so at the Joyce.

As we took our seats, we found ourselves facing a veritable wall of stage! We had to look up, way up, to see the dancers. An odd perspective perhaps, but we had terrific views of all the footwork.

As members of the studio company of the American Ballet Theater, all the young dancers in this group had auditioned for this coveted opportunity to perform and be further considered for full company membership in due course. They were the *crème de la crème* of young American ballet dancers. Ian had even thought this might be a group that would interest him. But the persistent thought among Ian's classmates was that they, the students at Canada's National Ballet School, were not good enough. They would not measure up to the lofty requirements and clear talent and training of their American counterparts. It was an inferiority that we could not comprehend. I often wondered if it had its genesis in the kids themselves–a kind of inbred, Canadian view. Although, to be accurate, at the NBS many students were not Canadians. There was a plethora of Americans and Asians when Ian was there. Perhaps, then, there was something in the way the school trained them that encouraged a kind of disingenuous modesty.

Whatever it was, Ian's feeling of inferiority was sorely shaken that evening, and we could not have been more gratified.

We watched a wonderful group of young dancers, but were struck by the fact that it was akin to watching the Spring Showcase of mostly grade 11 and 12 students at the NBS. The dancers here had already graduated from comparable schools. We were dumbfounded.

After it was all over it was obvious that Ian was suffering from a bit of cognitive dissonance, as it were. His strongly held notions of himself, his training and the wider world of ballet were turned upside down. He turned to us incredulously. "I actually *could* dance with them some day!" And he was right. Point to the parents!

In the grand scheme of things, it was clear that although we parents might have perceived a kind of Syndrome where the students working under a lot of physical and emotional stress might risk losing sight of their individuality, on balance the truth was just that we didn't really understand the way things worked in their world. They didn't see it the way we sometimes did; and we didn't understand the way things had to be. There was a hierarchy and there was ballet etiquette; both had to be respected.

We were not that skilled at respecting the ballet world etiquette, it seemed. In our defense it has to be said that it was often a bit like trying to find our way in a new city without a map. However, I'm certain that the school would have been more likely to think that we just didn't believe that the rules of etiquette were meant for us when we thought that other concerns trumped them: to whit, the travel plans.

It all started with our decision to spend spring break of the year Ian was in grade 11 in London. We had taken him there briefly some years earlier but had not been back since. It was his school's responsibility to train his mind and body and educate him for the specifics of his career. We felt strongly it was our responsibility to continue to show him a larger world and to expose him even to aspects of his own world beyond the confines of the National Ballet School, Toronto and even Canada as we had done the previous year in New York. We believed that it was our responsibility to teach him what became known comically in our family as life lessons. Sometimes the life lessons were as mundane as learning to clean a bathroom. At other times those lessons were infinitely more inspired and wonderful. We wanted to take him to Covent Garden to see the Royal Ballet, and because we had the means to do so, we made plans. He was delighted. We thought that his school would be delighted as well. We had formed the impression over the years that they valued this kind of exposure to the world. They did, sort of, and only if we were clear about the hierarchy involved in such decisions.

Every year parents were told the specific days and times that classes ended for breaks like Thanksgiving, Christmas, Spring Break, etc. We were exhorted not to make any plans for the child to have to leave school before that appointed hour. It was always difficult for those of us farther east since there would be limited flights available so late on any given evening, putting him home just before midnight, later if the flight was delayed. Indeed, if parents wanted to make earlier arrangements, the Artistic Director had to be contacted in advance. The problem was that such decisions were never fast enough. For years we worked within these parameters, trudging to the airport on countless occasions late at night through all kinds of inclement weather to pick Ian up from the last flight out of Toronto headed to the east coast. We rarely asked for an indulgence or have him miss a few hours of classes on a Friday afternoon before a holiday so that he could catch an earlier flight. However, whenever we did so–or even contacted the school for any other reason–the response was always slow in coming. I spent many days checking e-mails and voice mails for responses to the few queries I made in the early years. The responses always came eventually, but never within the time frames that are generally considered acceptable business etiquette. This time, we had to make the reservations many months in advance, and because we wanted to travel on points to defray the costs, we had to get those limited seats booked very early. When our travel agent calls and says there are seats available (we were using points for two and paying for the third), we have hours, if not only minutes to make a decision. The flights all left Toronto at such an hour that Ian would have to leave school a bit early. We didn't think that this was such a big issue; his classmates did it all the time. Presumably, though, their parents always asked for permission and waited for the response. We couldn't afford to wait.

So we took matters into our own hands. We decided that we'd follow the old military adage: it is easier to seek forgiveness than to get permission. In the ballet world, that may not be true.

March 16, 2006

Make no mistake about it–we have been chastised. We are planning the spring break trip to London–it necessitates Ian leaving school two or three hours early. But we have had the audacity to make the arrangements before asking permission of his artistic director. What? How could we? When the school can't tell us the schedule two days ahead of time, I seriously doubt if they could do it six months prior! And besides, we're his parents, damn it!

In her carefully worded e-mail, the artistic director goes around and around about Ian having to approach a director to "learn if there will be a problem in light of rehearsals etc." Well, that's illogical to my mind. It's now only two weeks before and she still hasn't a definitive answer. So, what's the point in asking? Art and I don't go to the school. We've made a parental decision and Ian is only doing what we are directing him to do.

Usually we're the ones caught between Ian and the school. This time he's caught between the school and his parents. Clearly, it's a kind of ballet world power thing that outsiders (us) couldn't possibly understand.

And so I e-mailed her again–a carefully worded missive.

"Dear Mavis,

Art and I certainly want to thank you for helping to (successfully) instill into Ian the kinds of skills that he needs to deal with future arrangements with artistic directors etc. You need to know that the arrangements for spring break were completely out of his control. Indeed, to his credit, he did tell us early on that you should be involved in the decision....

The decision was ours alone...As parents we have tried over Ian's years at NBS to comply with NBS expectations; however, in the kinds of lives we have, conflicts do occur from time to time and sometimes we have to make choices."

Oh, it was difficult. We did understand the need for Ian to respect such etiquette–it had both esoteric and practical ramifications. But we sometimes felt that our role as parents was not being respected in these kinds of situations. Were we being petulant? Perhaps a bit. I never believed that the school did these things with any malice intended, but rather that we were not complying with behaviour that is expected in the ballet world. (An orphan thing again, no doubt.)

I guess I always thought that my child's world would be a subset of my world. I never really had a conscious thought about this, as I suspect is the case with most mothers, until I realized that his world was so far from my own. I only had to learn to accept this reality.

TWENTY-TWO

...and then There Was a Prince

It takes an athlete to dance, but an artist to be a dancer.
–Shanna LaFleur

What does it take to be a prince? In the dance world, men often play the part of a prince in a traditional story ballet. (Think *Cinderella, Sleeping Beauty* and even *Romeo and Juliet*, although I've never been certain if Romeo was supposed to be a real prince in Shakespeare's story or just a prince-like character.) It occurred to me some time during my years as the mom of a male ballet dancer that being a truly memorable prince on stage required something deeper, something more than skilful technique, as if perhaps he held the role within his soul. And not all of them make it happen on stage. As an audience member you can see that, though. But if you try to say in so many words what it is that captivates you, it's tough to articulate.

When Rex Harrington neared retirement from his brilliant tenure as a principal dancer with the National Ballet of Canada, a number of newspaper articles included personal reflections about him by colleagues and others. Known by both audiences and ballerinas alike as a brilliant partner, Harrington had often been described as a kind of matinee idol; he was the original Sexy Rexy. The first time I saw the National Ballet of Canada's *Nutcracker*, he danced the lead. The moment the scrim rose and he walked across the stage sweeping, I knew that there was something about him. It seems that he had always had *it* and his fellow dancers knew it, too.

In 2004, on the occasion of Harrington's 20th anniversary with the company, the CBC interviewed fellow dancers, and the piece on him helped to uncover what it takes to be a prince. In addition to the requisite good looks some of those characteristics, it seems, include things like gentlemanly manners, a terrific ability to communicate–presumably with both his partners and the audience–intelligence and that unmistakable charisma, *presence*. Fellow dancer Patrick Lavoie said this: "Presence is so hard to describe, but when somebody has presence, they do nothing. They walk on stage and you notice them right away. You ask yourself, 'Why am I looking at this person and not somebody else?' That's what Rex always had."

This, I believe, is what it takes to be a prince. Over the years I watched these characteristics take form in my own young son. Would he be a star? I'm his mom, so of course he's a star to me. Would my own son follow in these large footsteps? Who could predict? But I was proud to see some of these princely characteristics develop as a result of Ian's hard work, his incredible teachers, the school's approach and his innate sense of himself.

The first time Ian was ever on a stage–as a four-year-old–it was clear that he was entranced by being up there. As time went on, it became increasingly clear that audiences loved seeing him there almost as much as he loved to be there. Art and I knew that there was something about him and others told us the same thing. It took some years before anyone at the NBS actually said this and I sometimes wondered if we were kidding ourselves. But finally, it began to emerge that we weren't so far off the mark.

April 15, 2004

What makes a mom cry when she reads her son's report card? I don't know what makes other moms cry, I only know me. I have Ian's report card in front of me–it arrived in the mail yesterday, two days after he has already returned to school for the final semester this year–grade nine. It says what we have always known: "He has the potential to develop into a dramatically powerful and charismatic performer." Charismatic–he has been that on stage since he was a very little boy. Now the ballet teacher sees it too. The potential is there.

It is so wonderful when your child's hopes and dreams, passion and dedicated work, begin to really gel and it's no longer left to you to wonder if what you see is simple parental prejudice–or so much more.

So the path toward becoming the prince had already opened, but it wasn't to be a smooth one for Mom and Dad.

If Dr. Meen and everyone else we met early on had left us with the distinct impression that we must ready ourselves for, among many other things, our child looking for a job out of grade 12, then somewhere along the way toward senior school and that far-off graduation something had happened. If we thought the changes in direction for planning things like exchanges gave us whiplash, then career planning gave us whiplash with a lingering pain in the neck.

Wednesday, March 8, 2006

Somewhere along the line the rules changed–and they forgot to tell us. Perhaps we weren't listening... It's been an insidious process of changing the company line that we should prepare ourselves for a child who will graduate from the NBS and go directly to his first job, to the notion that this is now a "two-part program" and that they all should prepare for one or two more years of study. At what point did the NBS program become inadequate for everyone? At what point did they stop meeting whose expectations? And if a student now believes that he will not be ready at graduation which is still over a year away, how could he possibly become ready with this mindset in his final year? And why weren't the parents of senior students who have been at the school since the days of the getting-ready-for-work mentality more a part of the process? Or even the kids for that matter?

When Ian began his studies at the NBS, his program was called Professional Ballet/Academic Program and was listed in the school calendar as the first program under the title, Full-time Programs. The second full-time program after this one was Intensive Dance

Program, affectionately referred to as IDP. This was billed as a post-secondary program for NBS grads, and equivalent grads from similar programs, providing "...supportive transition from basic training to full-time professional practice." We hadn't paid much attention to the nuances of what this might imply since it had not been suggested in any way that this was the normal course of events. So, our mindset developed. I'll admit it became fairly well entrenched in us, as it had been so difficult to move away from the idea that Ian would go to university in the first place.

That's what the calendar said in Ian's first year, and in the year he returned after the absence, and again in the following year. The year he entered grade 10, however, the calendar called the IDP program Intensive Dance Program (Advanced Post-Secondary Training). The newly worded entry said, "This program focuses on preparing dancers for entry into professional careers and is structured to provide a supportive transition..." A slight rewording from our point of view, but from the school's point of view it held a world of difference in its implications. The calendar also added that the NBS would make every effort to find "...professional work experience outside the school" for each student. This was quite different in emphasis. Yet before we found this calendar entry, nothing had been said to parents of kids whom it might affect–if, indeed, that was how it was intended. In fact, it wasn't until we neared the point when Ian would begin to consider audition opportunities for ballet companies that I even went back to the annual calendars and read this.

By the time the next calendar was published, the IDP program had become the Post-Secondary (Phase Two of the Professional Ballet Program). By this time it was 2005 and Ian was entering his penultimate year. Suddenly he was officially in a program called Ballet Academic (Phase One of the Professional Ballet Program). What were we supposed to think now? It wasn't exactly what we had signed up for–and evidently it wasn't what Ian had signed up for either. That was the year that they assigned him, for the second year in a row, a Russian ballet teacher with little teaching experience, who Ian had difficulty understanding on any level and who, by our parental estimation, had difficulty understanding Ian. We were perplexed by this assignment, but again felt they probably knew what they were doing despite all the times the previous year we'd had to deal with a distraught son who continued to say, "No, don't do anything." It was so frustrating as a mom, but I did as he asked. But this certainly made us wonder.

Here's what happened. The school has a wonderful career-planning continuum that starts at the beginning of the students' grade 9 year. At that time parents are invited to a meeting with the career planner and his assistants. The faculty member then in charge of the program was a wonderful man who had spent the latter part of his dance career as a principal dancer with a major ballet company. He was another of those so very dedicated, passionate faculty members whom we grew used to meeting around every turn at the NBS. We dutifully attended the meeting that year where the notion of any two-part program was not made clear. The information provided was helpful but general. We never went back to another such meeting since the agenda every year was the same. Moreover, it was our view that every student, just like everyone outside the ballet world, was an individual and that individual career planning would be in order. It was hard to even fathom the very idea of career planning, though, since Ian was still not quite sixteen.

As parents who knew our son quite well by that time, or so we continued to believe, we had instilled in him the mantra that it is better to shoot for the stars and miss than to shoot for the moon and hit it. With that in mind, we had supported his developing sense of himself. As the next year and a half unfolded, we found there was some kind of mould into which the school felt he should fit. I didn't know much about ballet, but I felt I knew a great deal about life and one of the things I knew for sure was that everyone has his or her own path. Indeed, by that time we felt strongly that if Ian needed another year of training, after seven years of NBS, if he wasn't ready then, another school would have to take over.

That second-to-last year was pivotal for me in understanding how the ballet world worked and how my pride in my son grew as he evolved into a mature, capable young man. Ian was still dealing with a teacher whose teaching technique was a daily stressor when he was cast in James Kudelka's piece. This seemed wonderful, but in February it all became a bit much and Ian had a bit of a crisis of conscience. He seemed to lose his sense of accomplishment. He called one night, distraught.

"I can't do ballet anymore."

Sometimes I really did not know what to say. If I had been in the room with him and been able to read his body language, all of this would have been a great deal easier. "What do you mean?" I said as evenly as I could manage.

"I just look ugly when I dance. My dancing is ugly. My body won't do what I want it to do."

There was no parent manual for this one. I wasn't sure what to do. Could he be right? Had something changed? A growth spurt he was having difficulty dealing with? I looked at Art, who mouthed to me, "Ask him if he wants to come home."

I ask. The answer, as expected, "NO."

The winter term was the longest and the hardest. We didn't really know what was going on. It could have been anything and the urge to intervene had never been stronger. We listened; we were there for him whenever he called. We went to Toronto for Music Night less than a month later. He was fabulous. The crisis seemed to have passed. We were then left to deal with the looming issue of the school's notion of what Ian ought to do after graduation and Ian's notion—two ideas not completely congruent. And then there was us. We were again in the middle.

When we went to Toronto for the Spring Showcase performance in May, the one where Ian had his debut solo performance, we also met with Mavis Staines regarding this career issue. She no longer intimidated us, but we were certainly concerned that it appeared that students were being forced into post-secondary training—right or wrong, but that was our perception—whether they needed it or not and whether or not it was their particular path to a career. In fairness to the school and artistic directors around the world who might have noticed a difference in graduates over the years, as a university professor I knew that they had reason to be concerned. I had personally noticed that over the preceding decade university freshmen had devolved into immature, narcissistic adolescents—clear products of their helicopter parents. Although this was a noticeable trend, it wasn't true of every individual. There are always exceptions.

The meeting with Mavis was, of course, very amicable.

Tuesday, May 23, 2006

There is no doubt in my mind whatsoever that the woman sitting across from us is very passionate about what she does and that she has taken to heart the comments of artistic directors around the world offered at a recent meeting. They seem to think that dancers are not ready right out of high school—a position they specifically told us to be prepared to face when we were earlier in our tenure here. However, the specific reasons for the change of heart and mind seem unclear to me. Is it that their dance skills are not up to the required level? Has something about the way the school does things changed? Is their conditioning wanting? Or is it some vague feeling that they are somehow not emotionally prepared to live and work? The latter would be quite insulting to parents since I believe it is largely our responsibility to impart those kinds of strengths. But it's probably true enough in many situations.

Who are we to stand in the way if Ian wants to give it a try? He is much better prepared for the bigger world than many of his classmates anyway. I can't comment on his ballet performance. I don't ever presume to have the expertise to do that!

She is not looking us in the eye, although it is clear that she is firm in her belief.

"What's the rush?" she says.

I imagine her thinking that we are pushing Ian. We assure her that the thrust comes from Ian, not us. She says she will tell a student (she does not specifically say that she will tell Ian) all the reasons that they should not move too quickly. We need something more specific. Will she forbid Ian to audition? Would she sabotage him? We are ruthless in our quest for real answers here. We know we are sticking our necks out, but we feel that it's the only way to get some answers.

She will not stand in his way. "However, I will not jeopardize my relationship with artistic directors."

I infer that she will not inflate her comments about any given student. Fair enough, I think. Neither would I inflate my recommendation of a student of my own at the university. We are now talking the same language. Honesty.

The whole issue of dancers' not being ready was a constant irritation at that juncture. Art was even more frustrated than I was, I think. But we both knew when to shut up. We had a niggling idea one of the reasons it might be so important now for students to stay on was so the school could increase its numbers to help pay for incredible new facilities that opened mere months before this meeting with Mavis. Coincidental, perhaps; a cynical view, no doubt. In our view, it was nevertheless worth considering.

By the end of the meeting, we were convinced that if Ian did not land an apprenticeship after Grade 12, we would help him find another school somewhere else in which he could complete his training. Mavis did tell us she would help with finding the right program. She then related a story of one student who had gone to Hamburg Ballet School because she wanted to enter their company. She detested her two-year stint but kept her eye on the prize for it would greatly improve her chances of entering the company. Improve her chances, but not guarantee it. It was so frustrating as a parent. It seemed to us that there was a kind of unspoken pecking order that we could not break. We were outsiders. I often wondered how we were viewed when all we really wanted was to help our child. That was one of those times I felt strongly that the school would certainly have preferred orphans.

So what does this have to do with the emergence of the prince? Lots. I was so proud of my son for he handled all this with grace and aplomb. When he was assigned Sergiu Stefanschi as his ballet teacher for his final year, Ian was elated. Feared by many students, Mr. Stefanschi was a legend. He had retired many years before from an outstanding career, the last years of which had been spent as a principal dancer with the National Ballet of Canada. Now he was a world-renowned master teacher. Formidable qualifications, indeed! Many of his protégées–Rex Harrington among them–had gone on to great careers. If Ian was excited, we were too. And it was a wonderful mentorship that developed. I guess if there is one teacher who stands out in my mom-memory as the one who brought out the best in Ian, it had to be this last one. Ian wouldn't even consider missing a class, almost to the point of ridiculousness in my view as a mother. I knew that there were times that year when Ian wasn't well or had a sore something or other, but he would not let Mr. Stefanschi know. He pushed through it.

During that final year, there were many ups and downs and further confusion for perplexed parents. The issue of auditions for companies became even more acute since we got the distinct impression that Ian was being pushed toward Europe. Art and I had often talked over the years about how wonderful it would be for ballet in Canada–not to mention parents like us–if more wonderful Canadian dancers could actually stay in Canada and populate the few ballet companies we have here. It would be so inspiring for Canadian children and so thrilling for audiences to see more NBS products rather than having them exported to Europe and beyond. Although it would have been our personal preference for Ian to stay in Canada, we also knew that these opportunities were few and that we really didn't have a say in it one way or another anyway. As a mother I was quickly getting to that point in life where I had to step aside. Ian was becoming a young man with decisions of his own to make.

In about January of that last year, Ian blurted out to us that if anyone should ask where he was going next year, we should say he would be in The Netherlands. Oh, I could feel the whiplash returning. His artistic director was headed to Europe and was taking Ian's audition DVD to the Dutch National Ballet. The thought was that, if they were truly interested in him, Ian would go to The Hague to the Conservatory for a while as an entrée into the company located in Amsterdam. With National Ballet of Canada auditions still a month off, we thought this was a premature decision. It was far too soon to be making such pronouncements, unless Ian had changed his mind about the auditions completely. As it turned out he had not, so I wondered why he was so adamant. Interestingly, it was at this juncture that we began to think he was suffering from Stockholm Syndrome! Small wonder.

By the end of January, Mavis had returned from Europe and told Ian, who of course had to relate it to us, that in the opinion of the artistic director at the Dutch National Ballet, the training for men in The Hague wasn't necessarily any better than what Ian could get in Canada. So, he might just as well stay at the NBS for a year. And by the way, if Ian wanted to go to The Hague to the Conservatory, the Dutch government insisted that foreign students appear in person for an audition. A DVD would not be good enough. He'd have to fly to Europe during spring break. Whiplash again. I was wondering when steam would start literally blowing from our ears.

But as they say, it's an ill wind that blows no good. Ian told us that it would be do or die for the upcoming auditions; so much was riding on it.

On Saturday, January 27, late in the afternoon the phone rang at home in Halifax. It was Ian. He was sitting on a streetcar in downtown Toronto. The audition for the six to eight apprentice positions available with the National Ballet of Canada had just finished. "It's the first time I actually thought I might have a fighting chance," he said.

So that was it. All that focus on going other places all came back to the old lack of confidence of so many of these wonderful, perfectionistic students. He was with several classmates who had also auditioned. It seems that he was the only one among them who felt as though he had had a good audition. He had not had much of a chance to look around at the other 80 or so auditionees, some from as far away as London's Royal Ballet School. He knew only that he felt good about himself.

It was a shining moment for a mother. Now all we had to do was wait with him for a letter. That letter would either be bad news, terrific news or limbo again. Some would receive a letter indicating that if they spent a year at the NBS in the post-secondary program, they might have a chance next year.

Another three weeks went by before Ian called to tell us the letter had arrived. "Dear Mr Parsons," he read to me over the phone, "Thank-you for your interest…it is my pleasure on behalf of Karen Kain to invite you to…" And the rest is history. He had won one of the coveted apprenticeships.

What a wonderful feeling for him. It told us, too, that we had not been so far off the mark as we watched our son dance. It was almost enough to make us forget how puzzled we were by Ian and the other two boys from the NBS who had won National Ballet apprenticeships dancing in the back row of the reel for *La Sylphide*, the chosen work for the spring showcase. We were so disappointed that there was not to be a showcase at all that year. If we had known that his big moment had been the year before, we would have invited people to join us in celebrating it. We had a reasonable expectation that the grade 12s would be showcased in their final year, and we were not alone. Many other parents voiced similar concerns to us at the time. But, again, there was nothing we could do and so we did nothing.

The prince truly emerged that year as Ian dealt with what appeared to us from afar to be a bit of jealousy from a few classmates. He never let his frustration and feeling of aloneness at the time get in the way of his sensitivity to others and the fact that many of them didn't yet know what they were going to be doing right after graduation. I felt deeply for him in that this was supposed to be the happiest year of his school life. It was one thing after another. My hope was that all of this would stand him in good stead as his career unfolded. It would probably not be the last time he was rewarded with something that passed others by. We all needed to learn that lesson in life.

As the song from the Broadway musical *Avenue Q* says, "Everything is only for now." The little boy who left home at eleven to pursue a dream was emerging as a prince, and now his ballet mom–and dad–weren't the only ones who thought so!

TWENTY-THREE

...til the Skinny Lady Speaks

[It] isn't over until the fat lady sings.

–anon

Opera's stereotype of the fat lady may have given rise to the oft-quoted aphorism that is generally interpreted to mean that you can't count your chickens before they hatch. Over the years in our house we knew that nothing ended until the skinny lady said so–and not metaphorically either. On a beautiful June day in downtown Toronto, the skinny lady spoke and it was over.

Tuesday, June 26, 2007

It's quiet in the house this morning. All I can hear is the lilting sound of bird calls and the occasional cry of a seagull. It's the first quiet moment I've had to sit alone with my thoughts in several days–the first time since the day we'd been awaiting for such a long time: Ian's graduation from the National Ballet School and my graduation from being a ballet mom. I don't think it really counts any more when your child is an adult and has embarked on his career.

How odd that sounds to my inner ear! He's an adult and although I'm still his mom, my role has reached a watershed and I've crossed over into another realm all together.

It's over. I can hardly believe it. It's a bitter-sweet time for a number of reasons. As I sit this morning with a coffee and Ian's year book ignoring those 89 e-mails that winked at me when I turned the computer on this morning, I haven't yet had the chance to really look at the book. As I turn page

199

after page of photos and memories of students, teachers and events, I feel a bit sad that an era is over–but only a little–a bit perplexed at the way it ended this year, and more than a bit relieved. In fact, when I really look inside my heart, my most prominent emotion is pride and happiness for Ian to have accomplished this and for it to be over for his parents. I'm also grateful to the NBS but, truly, I don't think I could have stood one more moment of being an NBS parent.

The evening before the formal graduation was memorable for one important reason for me as a mom: I found out that many of the highs and lows, the anger and confusion, the general feeling of powerlessness that I had often felt as a mom and that Art and I together had often felt as parents over the years indeed were not unique to us. After seven years, this was the first time I really had a feel for what other parents thought–save for the occasional lucid comment from Elizabeth, whose son had been three years ahead of Ian and had long since evaporated from the school horizon. The parents' gathering was an eye-opener for us.

We had been instrumental in planning this dinner, the first of its kind among parents of graduating students so we were told. In fact one of the moms, whose daughter was a long-time classmate of Ian, told us that she had been chatting with the artistic director earlier that day. Evidently the discussion ended with a comment on the event that evening that graduates were to attend without their parents. Reportedly Mavis asked, perhaps rhetorically, "And what are the parents going to be doing tonight?" When told that we were having our own dinner, she raised her eyebrows in what was interpreted as surprise–perhaps alarm? "Oh," was all she was reported to have said. She might well have been uneasy about the gathering since we had one final occasion to celebrate and, at the same time, commiserate about our feelings toward the school.

Art and I had decided we would sponsor a little reception prior to the event itself. That gave us a chance to stand around with a glass of bubbly and reminisce about our years involved with the school. Like us, a few parents had been associated with it for six or seven years; others had a more limited exposure. Much of the conversation revolved around how happy they all were that the kids were graduating–and not only because of their pride in their accomplishments.

During the dinner that followed, when I made a toast to our regaining our identities (we'd truly lost them when we began receiving mail addressed 'Parents/guardians of...'), it seemed I had not been alone in my consternation over this simple snub. Okay, it may have been for practical reasons on the school's part, but practicality doesn't always trump the maintenance of mutual respect and supportive relationships.

The highlight of the evening, though, was the slide show Art had painstakingly created over a period of several months in anticipation of this event. When we first broached the subject of such a celebration, we asked parents to send along digital photos they had in their archives of their children's experiences in relation to the school. And so they came. And they came. One evening a week before the event Art told me he had finished his 40-minute journey from the early days of those who had been there the longest to the most recent music nights and celebrations at residence and beyond. Some of the pictures were funny, others were poignant; some were formal, others were candid. Every child in the class was included, even those two students from Japan who had won scholarships to complete their last year of high school in Canada and had been there only since September.

A sound track from music nights over recent years accompanied the creatively shaped presentation. Art had painstakingly combed his music files to come up with the most appropriate and moving pieces. His selection criterion was that the pieces of music had to be sung by students in the graduating class.

The first song he chose was from an internationally themed music night production from just over a year before. The students had been in grade 11 and the music was a group rendition of a Nova Scotia folk song. "No one's in doubt that the children singing all too soon will be women and men..." So began the lyrics in four-part harmony. That sentiment was all too clear. The tears started flowing.

The music moved on through such material as "Seasons of Love" from *Rent*– "How do you measure a year in the life...?" (well, how *do* you?) and the appropriately named Billy Joel song "Movin' Out" from his Broadway show. By the time we got to "We Are the Champions" from the Queen's *We Will Rock You,* there was not a dry eye in the place–save for perhaps Art and me, desensitized by having seen the thing so many times. I was still moved, though, by the depth of the love and pride that was so evident in the parents. I sat a bit back, not to observe really, but to give better views for those who had not seen it before. However, it did give me a chance to take a bit of a bird's-eye view.

This bird saw the most committed and devoted parents any group of high school students could ever have. They sacrificed precious time with their children through critical years of their development. They gave moral and financial support, more often than not from a distance. They endured the puzzling edicts from the school. They learned when to intervene and when to heed a child's warning, "Please don't do anything, Mom! I just wanted someone to know about it." They juggled other family and business responsibilities with the school's unalterable schedule. They adapted quickly whenever the school changed its mind about something. Many of them had even dug deep into their pockets to provide extra support to the school itself in fundraising for wonderful new facilities. It was no longer important that the school know any of this. It was enough to know that, although each of our children might have had a different path, many of the tribulations along the way were the same.

The following day, a Friday, dawned sunny and beautiful in Toronto. The hot, humid turbidity had evaporated and left a pleasant day for a graduation where boys could be as comfortable in long-sleeved jackets as the girls were in strapless gowns. From the beginning it was a fashion parade. We spent forty-five minutes outside the academic building where photographers of all shapes and sizes, including one official one, snapped literally thousands of pictures for posterity. We did our share, that's for sure.

The group of twenty-four stunning teenagers on the front steps of the school, with the apparent gathering of paparazzi along for the ride, slowed pedestrians and drivers on busy Jarvis Street. Those who had missed the sign with the name of the school on the adjacent building must surely have wondered what group of celebrities they had just spotted. We all jockeyed for the best shots of individuals, of small knots of students and parents, and then of the inevitable group. It's funny. There were absolutely no teachers around. I had thought this would offer an opportunity for a few photos with them, to capture those memories as well, but they all seemed to have had other plans.

After what we felt was quite enough stargazing, Art and I made our way to the school theatre to await Ian's great aunt and uncle whom we had invited to the celebration. We all eventually took our seats and, true to NBS culture, the ceremony started–ten minutes late!

Unlike more traditional high school and university graduations where the graduates enter in grand procession accompanied by familiar march music, the curtain raised on a stage with two obvious camps: selected faculty members on one side and empty bleachers on the other. Ian had earlier told us that traditionally when the curtain rises on NBS graduation, students are already seated. He had had years of observation because all students in the school, from the youngest grade 6s to the upcoming graduates of the next year, were required to attend. Indeed, the main reason the ceremony started late this time was that the younger students weren't seated on time.

The Artistic Director stood at a podium at centre stage. She moved the microphone into position, smiled at the audience and began to explain that this class of unique individuals (Perhaps she meant uncooperative, individual non-traditionalists? Oh no, sorry, that would be us, the parents.) had decided to do something different. They wanted to make an entrance. So, they did. No surprise there.

They took their seats and the proceedings began.

I had sat through many graduation ceremonies–mine several times, my step-daughter's, my students'–too numerous to mention. I was never nervous. Why should I have been? Today was somehow different.

The Artistic Director, joined by the Academic Principal, began the formalities of handing out the diplomas. Graduates were given their moments in the spotlight as the artistic director spoke about each of them individually. Preparation of these unique speeches each year must have taken up quite a bit of her time, I was thinking. She must have kept notes and then thoughtfully prepared a paragraph or two to help the audience participate in each student's journey. It seemed a daunting task, but she was clearly up to it.

As I listened to the tributes to the graduates that afternoon, I was struck by the number of times she mentioned the struggles and the obstacles that each had faced. Indeed, there seemed to be an inordinate emphasis on the need to have overcome injuries. Some were still reeling from their injuries, not yet knowing if they would ever pursue a career in dance at all.

She came to Ian–my son and one of the proudest accomplishments of my life and yet not my whole life. She told a little story of when he first auditioned for the school. She told us that after the audition she had excitedly called the head of the junior school to tell her that she had just met an extraordinary little boy whom she truly hoped would accept their offer to come to the school. At the end she said that he had turned into a beautiful dancer. Ian looked pleased.

Then came the awards. It was no surprise that Ian was the winner of the musicianship award. Although other students had done well in music, no other student, in our minds at least, had so embodied the theoretical side coupled with an incredible ability to share that musical gift with the world. My mind slipped back to the very first music lessons Ian had taken, and I recalled that we had been told then that he was musically gifted. Those teachers had been right. I wondered if it was always as easy to predict.

Then came the ballet awards, some of them predictable, others extremely puzzling. I sighed realizing that I would get up from my seat and go on with my life, never really understanding much of what went on behind the scenes at this school that had been so much a part of our lives for so many years. Then we made our way to the dinner where at least we could share a glass of wine in celebration.

If we thought that the ceremony was perplexing, the dinner was more so and truly anti-climactic. We looked for the principal so we could say goodbye, but we never did find him, which led us to believe that he didn't appear at the dinner at all. No regrets were forthcoming; he just was nowhere to be found. The artistic director breezed past our table and Ian was disappointed that she didn't stop to speak. All we wanted to do at that juncture was to say thank-you for her mentorship of Ian, but she left very early so we couldn't. We were so proud of our son and his singular accomplishments.

We left Ian with his fellow graduates that evening after the dance so that they could spend one last night together. Then, rather than taking a taxi, Art and I both felt that we needed some air, both literally and figuratively. So we walked through the dark streets of Toronto on that evening in early summer shaking our heads. For something that had been so much a part of our lives for so long it was a strange feeling, made stranger by the fact that in the end we never did even begin to understand the inner workings of the institution. Perhaps it was better that way.

Over the years we had enjoyed so much about our forays into the world of the ballet and its elite inhabitants, even if we were really outsiders with our noses pressed against the glass. We watched this group of little kids grow into sophisticated, talented, beautiful adults. We learned to live as peripheral beings in much of our young child's life. We had learned how to shrug off things that we didn't understand and were clearly not meant to. A year earlier we thought that we would dearly miss the annual rituals of Parents' Day, observing classes, Music Night, Spring Showcase, summer choreographic workshops. It had become the rhythm of our lives. But we were tired and it was clearly time to move on.

As Theodore Geisel, better known to most of us as Dr Seuss; said, "*Don't cry because it's over. Smile because it happened.*"

We are smiling, in spite of ourselves.

EPILOGUE

What I Learned at the *Barre*

We are sitting at Il Fornello, a trendy little Italian restaurant a block from the National Ballet School. It is the end of summer school. Ian has spent the past four weeks here attending classes to keep in shape before he begins his contract as an apprentice with the National Ballet of Canada. That's only days away now.

We are waiting for him. He's late. It's not like him to be late so we order a glass of prosecco and toast to the end of an era. He has choreographed a piece that we will see on stage at the choreographic workshop presentation in a couple of hours.

I look at my watch. "Okay," I say to Art. "He's seven minutes late. [We'd joked to him that he had seven minutes grace]. I'll call him."

Art takes his phone and begins to scroll through his phone book to find Ian's new cell phone number. The phone rings in his hand before he has a chance to dial. Art glances at the picture that comes up. It's Ian.

"Dad," he says. "I'm at the corner of Church and Wellesley streets in a cab. I was hunted down by the library lady and she took my last five dollars to pay for my overdue library fine."

Art is on his way to bail Ian out–but not before we had a laugh and a toast to the NBS. Ian had graduated five weeks earlier and they were still on his case. We vowed to send them money to pay other grads' library fines forward.

I learned a lot about parenthood from becoming a mother to my son. The best teachers are often not where we seek them and as the old saying goes, "When the student is ready, the teacher appears." I was ready to learn when Ian appeared in my life. But being a mom is much more than giving birth to a child. Motherhood is a process, not an outcome. It is also never the whole of what a woman is, whether she realizes it or not. Being mom is only one layer of the onion of a woman, and being a ballet mom is just another layer that can be peeled off to reveal the heart.

Lest you think that being a ballet mom was my whole life, and at the risk of sounding self-important, just consider this. From the time Ian told us that he wanted to learn more about dance at age eight until he began his apprenticeship with the National Ballet of Canada ten years later, I did a lot of non-mothering kinds of things. I wrote three books and a raft of articles for academic and industry publications; I was promoted from associate professor to full professor at my university, a task in itself; I was inducted into my professional association's College of Fellows; I sat on several boards; I taught university students; I developed new courses. Well, you get the picture. I also learned to meditate in addition to my decades-long yoga practice. Art and I traveled often–sometimes with Ian but increasingly without him when his schedule would not permit. I had a very full life. But being a ballet mom was an experience that shaped my sense of what parenthood can and probably should be. Ballet mom doesn't define who I am, and never really did, but it was an unforgettable experience.

Every ballet dancer spends countless hours at the *barre*. In a way, so does a ballet mom. The dancer learns to move through his space; the mother learns to move through hers. That *barre* taught me different things than it taught my son; but make no mistake, it taught me a lot.

First, it taught me that every child is creative and, by extension, so is every person. I knew from the earliest days that my own child had a special connection to music. Every child is connected to something and finding that certain something is the key to a complete education. Moms are often the ones front and centre in the search.

But there can be minefields in trying to find that talent. I learned this from close observations of other ballet moms–and less so dads. That lesson is this: When a child's passion seems to echo your own–unfulfilled as it might be–be cautious about living vicariously through the child. Although my own passions were not mirrored in my son's directly, since I never wanted to be a dancer, I did want to be an actor at one time. I had to be so careful that my desire to be around all things performance-related did not get in the way of his finding his own way. For parents whose passion is dance and who did not fulfill that particular fantasy, it must be an even trickier highwire act. But there's another side to this as well.

I learned that it is equally as important to be vigilant of your own responses when a child's passion doesn't reflect your own expectations or dreams; a parent still has an obligation to respect the child's dream. This can be especially hard in the arts since practicalities like making a decent living wage loom large in a culture that pays its hockey players multiple millions and ballet dancers a pittance. When parents are highly motivated toward seeing their child do something in particular, whether it is similar to their own direction or a direction that they did not have the opportunities to pursue, it is fairly common to see those children pursuing things that don't excite them and often don't even reflect their most important talents. Billy Elliot's father had a lot of personal turmoil as he moved, grudgingly at first, toward accepting that his son was not going to be a coal miner, but rather a ballet dancer. Although we may have reached acceptance more easily because of our attraction to the arts, nevertheless the process was similar.

Then, when you do accept that the child is going to pursue his own path, at least get out of the way. But, it's more fun to educate yourself and be a part of it, no matter how peripheral. I had to learn a lot about the world of dance in general and ballet in particular. I started from a completely blank slate. Essentially I knew nothing. I'm still learning. However, I believe that this is a very important part of mothering–learning about your child's passions.

Educating yourself is clearly only part of it. That education can help you find the right mentor for your child, though. Even if the child's passion does reflect your own–not my personal experience– it's important for the child to have the right teachers. As I learned more about dance schools, I was able to find the one that would be right for Ian and in the process found him his earliest mentor. It's not something you can force, though. Just because mom thinks a particular teacher would be a good fit, the child will be the one to let you know whether or not you're right!

Another important lesson I learned: A mom and dad's support for the triumphs can never be any stronger than the support they need to give in times of disappointment. It's so easy to get excited about the successes. The path, however, is never smooth and straight. The disappointments are inevitable and that support needs to be there as strongly in times of difficulty as in times of achievement. As parents, I consider that we were incredibly lucky. Although the road was not smooth, as I look back I see that the ups and downs–particularly the downs–were not so severe as they were for many other parents. The disappointments, while significant at the time, pale in comparison to the triumphs. This may be the case with everyone.

I also learned that the experts can help lot, but in the end only a parent is a parent. If any of my lessons were learned the hard way, this was one. The constant push-pull between school and parent can be challenging in the most benign of situations. When the child's future looms large, the parent's role is important if only to provide perspective to a maturing adolescent. We could have left everything up to the school, and quite possibly things would have turned out the same. However, I firmly believe that my son needed to have a different perspective added to the mix so that in his last year or two of training he could make well-informed decisions. We didn't make the decisions for him–as tempting as it was–but we did provide counterpoint and it was both welcomed by him and used to his advantage.

Here's a big lesson I learned: a child's artistic pursuits will have a huge impact on the way your own life unfolds. Sure, a parent can take a completely hands-off approach, but if we had done that we would have missed so much fun. We allowed ourselves to enter into the flow, if only on the periphery, and our lives were enriched as a result. We met wonderful people; we traveled to fabulous places; we opened our eyes to a whole life that we would never fully be a part of, but it was thrilling in any case. And it will continue to have an impact.

As we move toward retirement, we'll look up Ian's classmates who have dispersed to all corners of the globe from Toronto to New York to San Francisco to Houston to China to Germany. We will look for opportunities to see them perform whenever we can.

One of the final lessons I learned is a terrific one for my life in general and something that Art has often said to me over the years: Expect the unexpected. Just when you think that all is settled, the artistic life of the child throws you a curve. Flexibility is the key to being able to cope with whatever comes along with humour and equanimity.

The final lesson I learned fairly early, a mantra that kept this ballet mom sane: *Prepare the child for the path and not the path for the child.* The path is already laid out. I see so many parents who are trying to lay that path for their children, and I see so many young adults who are unhappy with the path they are on, or have been manipulated into.

At the final dinner with the other parents of graduating students that memorable June, Art and I chatted with one of the other moms, a successful lawyer with a prestigious position. Her daughter was both a promising dancer as well as a truly brilliant student academically. In fact, in trying to make up her mind about what direction to pursue, the daughter had applied to university and been offered the largest scholarship available to freshmen. The mother was worried that her daughter could not make a living as a dancer, although she sensitively acknowledged that this was a passion she had pursued through to graduation from Canada's National Ballet School with a view to a ballet career. When the mom told us that she herself had been a pianist and had two music degrees–all before going to law school, Art astutely asked her, "What would you rather be doing now at this point in your life? Practicing law or playing piano?"

She didn't even have to think about it. "Playing the piano," she said. She smiled.

I had a deep feeling from my very earliest years as a mother that my child belongs not to me but to the world; I just wasn't sure what this might mean. I used to think it is because he's supposed to pursue a very public life as a performer. Now I think it's true for everyone's children. They are not really ours. It is our privilege to care for them, to love them unconditionally, and to nurture them into adulthood. But they–and we–all belong to the world.

Let your children go if you want to keep them.
–Malcolm Stevenson Forbes